Lochaber

A Historical Guide

Lochaber

A Historical Guide

Paula Martin

Birlinn

First published in 2005 by
Birlinn Limited
West Newington House
10 Newington Road
Edinburgh EH9 1QS

www.birlinn.co.uk

ISBN10: 1 84158 241 7
ISBN13: 978 1 84158 241 2

British Library Cataloguing in Publication Data
A catalogue record for this book is available from the British Library

Typesetting and origination by Brinnoven, Livingston
Printed and bound by Bell and Bain Ltd, Glasgow

CONTENTS

ACKNOWLEDGEMENTS

First of all I would like to thank Richard Oram, the series editor, who suggested that I write this book. He also read and commented on the historical section, and helped the text take shape. My husband Colin accompanied me on several outings to explore Lochaber, and took many of the photographs. Our son Peter very kindly helped out by turning my photographs into line drawings; our other son Edward helped with advice on computing and scanning. I am particularly grateful to Jennie Robertson for permission to reproduce her drawings of Uladail.

My thanks also go to Hugh Andrew and Andrew Simmons of Birlinn for their tolerance when deadlines were missed. I enjoyed exploring Lochaber district while writing this book, and would like to thank all the helpful and friendly people I met while driving and walking around the many fascinating and beautiful corners of the area which but for this book I might never have visited.

HOW TO USE THIS BOOK

The first section consists of a historical narrative. The second is made up of twelve thematic gazetteers, with numbered entries. Numbers in brackets in the text, and after Plates and Figures, refer to gazetteer entries. Plates, maps and figures are also referred to at relevant places in both text and gazetteers.

LIST OF PLATES

1. Clach-a-Charra standing stone, Onich (1.9). (Colin Martin)

2. One of the kerb cairns at Claggan, Morvern (1.1). (Colin Martin)

3. Free-standing cross, Iona School, fourteenth–fifteenth century, Kiel, Morvern (3.3). (Colin Martin)

4. Lower part of another cross depicting a bishop, Iona School, fourteenth–fifteenth century, Kiel, Morvern (3.3). (Colin Martin)

5. An arch from the medieval church at Kiel, Morvern, surviving in the graveyard (3.3). (Paula Martin)

6. A West Highland galley – detail from a late-medieval grave slab, Kiel, Morvern (3.3). (Colin Martin).

7. Cill Choirille (St Cyril), Glen Spean (3.2). (Colin Martin)

8. Relocated gate from the fort at Fort William, 1690 (5.8). (Paula Martin)

9. Inverlochy Castle (4.7). (Colin Martin)

10. Castle Tioram, Moidart (4.11). (Colin Martin)

11. Eilean Munde, burial isle in Loch Leven (3.11). (Colin Martin)

12. Gravestone on Eilean Munde commemorating a man who killed a dragoon at Prestonpans in 1745 (3.11). (Colin Martin)

LIST OF ILLUSTRATIONS

(All by Peter Martin unless stated otherwise)

1. Clan Cameron Museum, Achnacarry (8.1)

2. The 'Ballachulish goddess' (from the original report of the discovery in *Proceedings of the Society of Antiquaries of Scotland*) (1.21)

3. Inverlochy Castle from the north-west (from MacGibbon & Ross, *Castellated and Domestic Architecture*)

4. Ardtornish Castle from the west (from MacGibbon & Ross, *Castellated and Domestic Architecture*)

5. Free-standing cross, Kiel, Morvern

6. A Highland ring-brooch, found on the wreck of HMS *Dartmouth*

7. Parliamentary Manse, Acharacle (5.1)

8. Engraving of the 'Floating Church' moored off Strontian (from Brown, *Annals of the Disruption*)

9. 'Preaching at the Sea Side', a frequent scene in the early days after the Disruption (from Brown, *Annals of the Disruption*)

10. View of the fort at Fort William (after an eighteenth-century watercolour)

11. Kinlochaline Castle from the south-west (from MacGibbon & Ross, *Castellated and Domestic Architecture*)

xiii

LIST OF MAPS

INTRODUCTION

Lochaber is a sparsely populated area, remote but romantic, centred on Fort William. It contains no medieval burgh, no major monastic site, and for its size, not even many castles. There are only two National Trust for Scotland properties (Glencoe and the Glenfinnan Monument), and two Historic Scotland properties (Inverlochy Castle and Bridge of Oich). However, it does include the highest mountain in Great Britain (Ben Nevis, 4406 ft/1344 m, though it was only in 1870 that it was confirmed as the tallest), the deepest lake in the British Isles (and the seventeenth deepest in the world) (Loch Morar, 310 m), and the most westerly point of the British mainland (Ardnamurchan Point). Daniel Defoe described Lochaber as a 'mountainous barren and frightful country . . . full of hideous desert mountains and unpassable'. Much of the land surface is mountain or bog, and its coastline is indented by long sea lochs, while the interior contains some extensive fresh water lochs, the largest of which are Loch Morar (26.7 square kilometres) and Loch Shiel (19.6 square kilometres).

The name Lochaber first appears in Adamnan's *Life of St Columba* (written *c*.690), referring to the region bordering the loch or bog of Apor (the Gaelic Aber or estuary). It probably refers either to the top of Loch Linnhe, or to a possible loch, later a bog, east of Banavie. Much of the scattered population of Lochaber has always lived close to its long and sheltered coastline, and until the last 200 years most communication was by water. One local minister in the 1790s claimed, probably correctly, that Tahiti and other Pacific islands were better surveyed than parts of the west coast of Scotland. Only a few intrepid travellers came here before the nineteenth century, when roads, steamboats and then the railway rapidly opened up the area to tourism. Attempts to introduce new industries during the twentieth century had mixed success, but the population, having declined for almost two centuries, has now stabilised. Perhaps a better understanding and demythologising of the past may help towards developing a sustainable economy for the future.

Geology and Natural Resources

Most of the Highlands consist of metamorphic rock (rock that has undergone transformation by natural agencies, usually as the result of volcanic activity) with patches of granite. Some of the geology is impressive. The western end of the Ardnamurchan peninsula, for example, is the crater of a long-extinct volcano, its circumference almost too vast to comprehend except from the air. The Great Glen is a geological fault cutting right across Scotland from Loch Linnhe to the Moray Firth. While the columnar basalt cliffs of Lochaber are not as spectacular as those on Staffa, those east of Ardtornish Castle on Morvern have waterfalls which are blown upwards by strong south-westerly winds: 'just when about to dash in sparkling fury over the giddy precipice, they are interrupted in their course; uplifted by the opposing gale and showered backwards, a dense cloud of foaming spray' (*New Statistical Account*).

In the words of the minister of Kilmallie in the 1790s, Ben Nevis 'attracts the attention of all curious travellers'. The parallel roads of Glen Roy, once believed to be the work of the mythical giant Fingal, were identified by John Macculloch in 1817 as being ledges which had once been the shorelines of a loch, created by water held back by the glacier which filled Glen More and blocked the entrance to Glen Roy. As the glacier receded, the water level fell, creating the series of three shorelines. Debris from glaciers also accounts for the mounds or 'drumlins' encountered on the valley floors, and it was glaciers which deposited the large isolated boulders of non-local origin, called 'erratics'. When glaciers descended a steep slope they often gouged out hollows at their back, known as 'corries'. On Rannoch Moor the forces of glaciers have scoured the granite, which, though hard, was softer than the adjacent rock, down to a flat wasteland. Glencoe is a classic U-shaped valley carved by a glacier.

There is little good arable land, a reasonable amount of pasture, including the area of salt marsh at the head of most sea lochs, and much mountain, moor and bog. Simple buildings of all periods have until relatively recently used wood (coppiced poles, or wattle) or turf blocks for walls, and turf, heather or other vegetable materials for roofing. It was the landowners during the eighteenth century who started to demand that buildings be made of stone, as they preferred to sell their wood, resenting its traditional use for housing by their tenants, and in some cases apparently failing to understand that its use had been sustainable. Better quality buildings used imported stone which could be cut into blocks, and slate for roofing. Timber for larger roof trusses also had to be imported, as did lime for mortar and plaster. Most of this would have been transported by sea, and for any site away from the coast the costs of land transport from the nearest harbour will have been very high.

There is plenty of local building stone, but much of it is difficult to cut to shape. Once building in stone became the norm, therefore, many walls were constructed of random rubble. Others used the largest blocks to make rough courses, filling the gaps with much smaller stones (a technique developed out of necessity, but by the later nineteenth century used decoratively). Areas of granite, such as both sides of Loch Linnhe, were exploited particularly in the nineteenth century when machine cutting made granite both easier to use and very desirable. The slate deposits at Ballachulish provided roofing material for much of Scotland. The Ballachulish deposits, however, like most Scottish slate, contain cubes of pyrite which eventually rust and leave holes. Another resource was marble. In the words of one local minister in the 1790s, 'what a pity it is, that such sums of money, should be sent every year to foreign kingdoms for marble, when our own country abounds with all kinds of stones, of the very best quality, necessary for ornamental architecture'. At the head of Glen Roy was a quarry specialising in quern stones (for grinding corn by hand), examples of which have been found over a wide area. At Inninmore, on the Morvern shore, are wasters from the quarrying of both millstones and gravestones.

There are a few small outcrops of coal in the Lochaline area, and near Ardslignish in Ardnamurchan, but they never proved commercially viable. John Knox in 1786 noted that 'copper has been discovered in the Highlands, but not in sufficient quantities to defray the expense of working. Iron stone abounds in many places; and lead mines have long been wrought with success.' Lead was found in the area around the head of Loch Sunart, and in Glen Nevis and Inverscaddle. It was extensively mined above Strontian, and the workings later also produced strontianite and barite. There was a short-lived copper mine at Tearnait, in Morvern. There is limestone in Kilmallie, Ardgour and Morvern, which was processed in the late eighteenth and early nineteenth centuries for use as fertiliser. Seaweed was also used as a fertiliser, and particular types of seaweed were gathered, dried and burned to make 'kelp', an alkali used in the manufacture of glass and soap.

Climate and health

Very useful sources for how people lived are the *Old Statistical Account*, compiled in the 1790s, and the *New Statistical Account*, compiled in the late 1830s and early 1840s. Both involved the minister of every parish sending in a description of the parish and its people. The minister of Glenelg in the 1790s claimed that 'the constant but moderate exercise, which is necessary for herding the cattle, and the sea-air enjoyed during the fishing-seasons, are favourable to health'. But the minister of Kilmallie pointed out that 'to the dampness of the air, may, no doubt, be attributed the frequency of the rheumatism . . . and since people have ceased to wear flannel shirts, it is become much more general.' There had been some resistance to inoculation against smallpox, but that had recently been overcome. However, the presence of a garrison at Fort William had brought venereal disease to the area.

But one minister claimed that 'the frequent rains, together with the inundation of the rivers. prove so destructive as to render the crops sometimes insipid and useless'. Most travellers commented on the heavy rainfall in the area. Their discomfort was usually enhanced by other difficulties encountered on their travels, such as poor roads and the very primitive accommodation and facilities offered by the few inns.

Population

The modern administrative district of Lochaber consists of the south-western part of Inverness-shire and the northernmost part of Argyllshire, both large counties, containing a wide range of landforms and settlements. Lochaber, defined by geography more than by administrative boundaries, and far from the county towns of Inverness and Inveraray, has its own natural focal point in Fort William. The Inverness section consists of the districts of Knoydart and Morar from the parish of Glenelg, but not Glenelg itself (which held about half the population); the whole parish of Kilmallie (a small part of which is in Argyll); and the whole parish of Kilmonivaig. The Argyll part consists of the peninsulas and parishes of Ardnamurchan and Morvern, together with Ardgour and Appin, which was the northernmost part of the parish of Lismore and Appin. West Highland parishes were vast. Kilmallie, the largest parish in Scotland, was 60 miles by about 30, covering nearly 600 square miles, Kilmonivaig was 60 by 20 miles. The huge parish of Ardnamurchan divides naturally into five areas – West Ardnamurchan, centred on Kilchoan, Sunart to the east; and Moidart, Arisaig, and South Morar to the north.

The population of the Highlands increased rapidly towards the end of the eighteenth century. There were a number of reasons for

Table of Population

Parishes	1755	1790s	1801	1831	1861	1891	1921	1951	1981
Argyll									
Ardnamurchan (total)	5,000	4,542							
Ardnamurchan (Argyll portion)			2,664	3,311	2,687	2,004	1,369	948	850
Lismore & Appin	2,812		3,243	4,365	3,595	3,135	3,787	2,505	1,494
Morvern	1,223	1,764	2,083	2,137	1,226	820	590	460	341
Inverness									
Arisaig & Moidart			2,165	2,358	2,013	1,602	1,375	1,002	719
Glenelg	1,816	2,746	2,834	2,874	1,843	1,503	1,643	1,486	1,209
Kilmallie	3,093	4,225	4,520	5,566	4,272	4,205	3,624	6,248	10,818
Kilmonivaig	2,995	2,400 (estd)	2,541	2,869	2,276	2,205	1,769	3,053	3,076
Total			20,050	23,453	17,912	15,474	14,157	15,702	18,507

this, including the growing of potatoes, which produced a greater yield per acre than grain crops. There was also the extra employment created by the kelp industry, and improvements in health, notably inoculation against smallpox. Despite voluntary emigration, 74 per cent of the parishes on the west coast experienced a population growth of over 25 per cent between 1755 and the 1790s. This was too much for the land alone to support, and after the collapse of the kelp industry in the 1820s, and in the absence of any other major economic activity other than farming, something had to be done. The desire of landowners to make their estates pay led to the introduction of flocks of sheep, displacing some tenants and many cottars, who often paid no rent. Some stayed on, forcibly resettled along the coast, often on poor-quality land, while others chose or were forced to emigrate, either to the rapidly industrialising towns and cities of the central belt of Scotland, or to the colonies, first to North America, then from the 1850s increasingly to Australia and New Zealand. As can be seen from the table above, the wholly rural parishes continued to decline in population until the 1950s, though are holding their own today, and possibly even growing slightly. The population of Kilmallie, however, reflects the steady growth of Fort William and its suburbs.

Archaeology and history

Archaeology, and history up to the mid eighteenth century, are covered in the introductory chapters. History after that date is covered in the thematic chapters. Both archaeological and historical remains are covered in the Gazetteer. Wherever you walk, you will come across evidence that the land has been more intensively inhabited and cultivated in the past, from prehistory through to living memory. There is little in this area which appears in general books as outstanding examples of its type, whether prehistoric site or country house, but this in no way negates the historical importance of the remains, and the need to understand what they can tell us about our own past, and about how this landscape has been used and changed.

The monuments have to be appreciated within their landscape setting. This was a land which could not be tamed. Landowners with ambitions for improving their grounds had to work with the landscape, and use views of or from their grand houses as part of their impact. Sites listed in the Gazetteer are those where there is something to see, and which are visible from the road, or reasonably easy of access. For those wishing to explore one part of Lochaber in more detail, the best source on historical and archaeological sites is CANMORE, the database kept by the Royal Commission on the Ancient and Historical Monuments of Scotland, and available on-line (www.rcahms.gov.uk), or the Highland Sites and Monuments Record (www.ambaile.org.uk/smr/index.jsp). The SCRAN database (www.scran.ac.uk) can provide more images of the buildings and landscapes described in this book, and also old photographs, for example of slate quarriers at Ballachulish. Maclean, *Around Lochaber*, is another source of old photographs.

This book is aimed at those who wish to explore the area, and to get a feel for the landscape and its past. It is always worth making the effort to leave the main roads and explore the minor roads or tracks, or to explore by water. However, although visitor centres and museums have not been highlighted, that is not to say that they

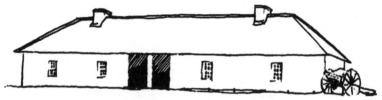

Fig. 1. Clan Cameron Museum, Achnacarry (8.1)

may not have something to add to the intrepid visitor's experience, and they are at least dry and free from midges. The main museum, and very well worth visiting, is the West Highland Museum in Fort William. There are others which are smaller or more specialised, including the Mallaig Heritage Centre, the lighthouse centre at Ardnamurchan Point, the Folk Museum in Glencoe village, the Railway Museum at Glenfinnan, the Clan Cameron Museum at Invergarry (Fig. 1), and the Commando Museum at Spean Bridge. Both the National Trust for Scotland properties, Glencoe and Glenfinnan, have visitor centres.

Note on access

Every site in the Gazetteer is given its Ordnance Survey map number (1:50,000 series) and a six-figure grid reference. Not all the sites listed are easily accessible, though anything included in the 'Must See' section is open to the public, reasonably easily accessible, or visible from the road. Please observe the Countryside Code; in particular, leave gates as you find them, and bring all your litter home. On single track roads, please do not park in passing places.

The best time to visit the Highlands, in terms of weather, is May and June. This is also a good time for wild flowers. From May to September you may encounter midges. Exploring off the road is made harder from June to October by bracken, which can often hide the remains of prehistoric cairns or cleared villages. If you go walking without being well covered up, you risk picking up ticks, which are present all the year round, but more numerous in spring and summer.

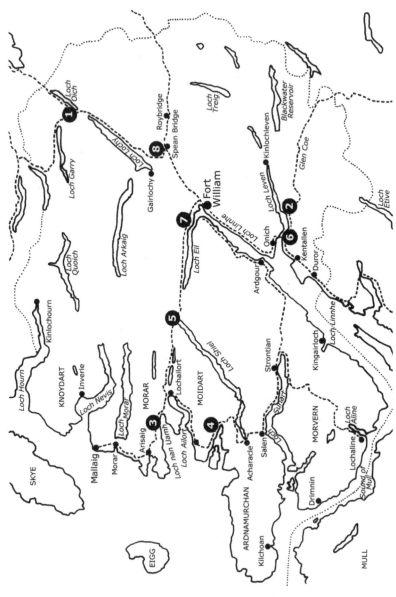

Map 1. Lochaber, showing the major roads and settlements, and the Lochaber district boundary

PART I

1. PREHISTORY

Recent research has yielded much new evidence about Scottish prehistory, and demonstrated a far more complex picture, with technological developments being introduced more gradually than was previously thought, and with greater regional variations. In simple terms, however, the picture remains the same – the first immigrants after the ice retreated were hunter-gatherers (Mesolithic) who gradually turned to settled agriculture (Neolithic), and then stone tools were gradually supplemented by bronze (Bronze Age) and then iron (Iron Age). For some periods we have evidence about settlements, in other periods more evidence survives about burial practices, ritual sites or defensive constructions. Some of the remains from prehistory, such as brochs and hill forts, still make a dramatic impact on the present-day landscape. Others, however, are less obvious and more ephemeral. While Lochaber does not have any spectacular stone circles or major hill forts, there is plenty of evidence of a humbler nature, such as cairns and standing stones.

Mesolithic

There is no firm evidence of the presence of people in Scotland at the end of the Palaeolithic (Old Stone Age), and most of the country was still covered by ice. After the end of the last Ice Age, prehistoric peoples quickly spread over the whole of what is now Scotland, and traces of their activity can be found in many places. The earliest definite residents were from the Mesolithic (Middle Stone Age) period, from about 7500 BC or quite possibly earlier. They were hunter-gatherers, who moved around the countryside, probably to a cyclical pattern, catching animals and fish, and exploiting wild fruits and fungi in season. Some sites provide evidence that they caught deep-sea fish, which must mean that they had sea-going boats. They certainly travelled to or lived on islands.

In some areas, such as the west coast of Scotland, they were able to make use of the natural shelter provided by caves. The country would probably have been heavily wooded, and woods are dangerous, as wild animals can be close by yet invisible. Quite apart from the availability of caves, open coastal areas may have been the easiest and safest places to make temporary camps. Apart from cave sites, Mesolithic sites which have been excavated using modern archaeological methods have demonstrated traces of posts having been set in the ground in irregular patterns, presumably representing tents or similar temporary structures, with wooden frames covered with skins or branches. Sometimes pits are found, or the sites of hearths. The first indication of a Mesolithic site is usually the presence of small worked flints, called microliths, or the waste products from their manufacture. Also found around the coast are middens (piles of waste material) containing shells, and sometimes animal and fish bones, and vegetable debris such as nut shells and seeds. Little else is known about the Mesolithic way of life, social structure or religious beliefs. But they seem to have lived in harmony with their environment, not changing it as later farmers would do.

At this early period Scotland was still joined to Denmark by an area of land known as 'Doggerland', now represented by the Dogger Bank, a major shallow area in the North Sea. During the Mesolithic period the land mass rose as the weight of ice was removed, but sea level also rose as the sea absorbed the melted ice. This led to fluctuations in the levels of both sea and land, but the end result was that the land rose up more than the sea, and around most of the coast of Scotland can still be identified one or more 'raised beaches', the result of the rising of the land in relation to the sea. It is on the first (lowest) raised beach that Mesolithic remains are often found.

Sites in the West Highlands with important clusters of remains include Oban, Oronsay and Rum. In Lochaber, shell middens have been found on the little island of Risga (2.24), in Loch Sunart, excavated in the 1920s, along with tools of stone, bone and antler, one piece of which has been dated to about 4000 BC. Evidence has also been found from several other sites in Ardnamurchan, both on the coast (such as Sanna Bay), and inland, and one coastal site in Morvern (Acharn). Other places, including forestry plough furrows, have yielded stray finds, but few have been excavated. On some of the Ardnamurchan sites have been found stone tools made with a distinctive bloodstone from Rum, which is 30 kilometres away across the sea. This must indicate either the ability to travel to acquire raw materials, or, more probably, some form of trading network. Much of Lochaber is far from ideal territory for hunter-gatherers, being rocky and barren.

Neolithic

Around 4000 BC farming seems to have been introduced, and this allowed people to settle in one area rather than living a nomadic life. Apparently spreading gradually from western Europe, this new farming lifestyle spread relatively quickly to every corner of Scotland. Neolithic farmers grew wheat and barley, and kept cattle, sheep and goats, and pigs. They probably still gathered nuts and berries as their ancestors had done, however, and they certainly supplemented their diet by fishing. In order to carry out their farming they must have cleared some of the native tree cover, though how much is open to debate. Not only did land need to be cleared to grow crops, but wood was needed for building homes and creating enclosures to separate crops and animals, as well as for smaller domestic objects. Grazing animals, however, impede the regeneration of trees, so the tree cover would be continually receding. But grazing animals also provide manure which is necessary if arable land is to be used repeatedly. There is evidence that a combination of deforestation, erosion and overcropping led to some soils being quite rapidly depleted, and some lochs filling up with silt.

Lochaber

Surviving evidence from this period includes stone axes, both everyday tools and what appear, from their quality and lack of evidence of use, to have been ceremonial objects. Other finds include stone beads, and the post-holes left behind by timber buildings. In Orkney, where the stone naturally splits into large slabs, and wood is scarce, stone buildings survive from this period, as for example at Skara Brae. The most obvious and dramatic evidence that Neolithic people have left us, however, is their burial and religious sites. These may well be statements of territory and ownership, more important to people who are settling on and claiming particular areas of land. Once again, the most spectacular of these are to be found elsewhere in Scotland, as at Maes Howe in Orkney. Among these apparently religious monuments are standing stones, both single and in lines and circles. Towards the end of the Neolithic period there seems to have been a change from large communal ceremonial monuments to smaller-scale, more individual constructions. Surviving evidence in Lochaber is slight, though there are cairns, some with central chambers, and some with kerbs of large stones. There are also stray finds of stone axes.

Bronze Age

The next phase of man's history is when, from about 2000 BC, metalworking skills reached the Neolithic farmers, and they learned to mix copper and tin (later including lead) to make bronze. At first this precious metal was only used to make small items such as daggers, and their metalworkers also made gold jewellery. Whether the Bronze Age culture represents an invasion of new people, as used to be believed, or just the absorption of new influences, burial patterns also changed. Single burials are found in stone cists, and later on cremations also appear, with the ashes buried in earthenware jars. Other evidence from this period includes hut circles and burnt mounds, made of shattered stones which had been heated up and then plunged into water. Their purpose is unclear. One suggestion is that the stones were used to heat water for cooking, another that they heated water for a form of sauna. There is no hard divide between the Neolithic and the early Bronze Age, with many practices, such as the construction of burial cairns, continuing.

During most of the prehistoric period the climate seems to have been warmer than it is now. There is evidence that Bronze Age farmers cultivated upland areas which have not been farmed since. Around 1300 BC there seems to have been a change to colder and wetter weather. The Late Bronze age seems to have seen changes in methods of agriculture, including an increased use of animals for carrying or pulling. Sheep, and the wool they produced, also seem to have become more important. The colder wetter weather led to the growth of peat, and the reduction in the area which could be farmed successfully. This reduction in available land seems to have led to a more unstable and warlike society, as evidenced by fortified structures, as well as bronze weapons. Once again, these changes used to be seen as the result of an invasion, but modern theory tends towards gradual assimilation of new customs, perhaps introduced by a small number of immigrants. By the end of the Bronze Age, Scotland seems to have been under the control of a warrior aristocracy, who built the first hill forts.

From the Neolithic and Bronze Ages in Lochaber there are few standing stones. The cup-and-ring markings, which are so distinctive a feature of the landscape of south and mid Argyll, are hardly found in this area. There are some cup-marks on Risga (Ardnamurchan, 2.24), and at some other places, but on rocks close to the high tide mark. These are usually classified as much later holes for grinding up or storing fishing bait, as for example on Eilean Rubha an Ridire (Morvern) or at Glenborrodale (Ardnamurchan). But there is probably more evidence to be found. In 1981 at Dail na Caraidh, near the junction of the rivers Lochy and Lundy (NN 129 764: OS 41) sixteen bronze axes were exposed by erosion, and subsequent excavation revealed another two axes, six daggers, and other Bronze Age material (now in Inverness Museum).

Iron Age

Whatever the reason, the next phase, known as the Iron Age, from around 700 BC, involved the introduction of the 'Celtic' language, new fortifications, and iron-working. There is also evidence for wider trade and foreign contacts. It was these peoples who in southern and eastern Scotland faced the Roman invaders, and generally seem to have learned to live with them. The Romans invasion did not reach this area, and though there is some evidence of trade and contacts between the Romans and the rest of Scotland in many places, including southern Argyll and Skye, there is little or nothing from Lochaber itself.

The wide variety of settlement types and defensive structures may well signify social fragmentation. Compared with the Bronze Age, there is an absence of ritual monuments, but a presence of dominant constructions such as brochs (mainly in the north and west), duns, hill-forts and crannogs. Brochs are more than one storey high, with double-skinned walls often with passages or stairs between the two walls, and a single low entrance. Duns are enclosures of similar shape and size, though they may be very irregular where they are built to fit a rocky outcrop. Unlike brochs the walls are usually single, and appear to have been less high, but they were thick, and in some cases interlaced with timber. When such ramparts were set on fire, the effect of the heat was to destroy the timber but through it to penetrate the stone and vitrify it, that is to say, to turn the stone into a glass-like substance. It has been established that such an effect was unlikely to be the result of accidental burning, but must have been intentional, perhaps a deliberate act marking the overthrow of the individual or tribe to whom the fort had belonged. Timber-lacing seems to have gone out of fashion, perhaps because of shortage of timber, and thick walls were subsequently built with a rubble core. Duns can date anywhere from the seventh century BC to the third century AD. Most of these fortified structures are found on or near the coast, which may imply a threat from the sea, but may just relate to the fact that some of the best land was on the coast, and needed protecting from other local landowners or tribal leaders. There are no brochs in Lochaber, and the main surviving monuments are vitrified forts and duns.

Another distinctive structure dating to the later Bronze Age or Iron Age (though sometimes reused much later) is the crannog. These were artificial or semi-artificial islands, usually in inland lochs, usually near the shore and sometimes linked to it by a narrow causeway. The classic crannog was built by driving a circle of oak piles into the bed of the loch and filling the area between them with stones. On top was built a typical 'roundhouse' or 'wheelhouse', a circular house with a central hearth, and probably partitions to create 'rooms' or distinctive working areas around the edge. It had a conical thatched roof, and would have looked just like houses on dry land. But there is also evidence for stone houses built on natural islets. The function of crannogs has long been debated. While they provided protection from wild animals, they were not particularly defensible from human attack. But they would have saved wasting good agricultural land by building on it, would have provided a platform for fishing, and from which boats could be launched, or may simply have been thought to be cleaner and healthier than living on land. Several crannogs survive in Lochaber. Some were discovered when lochs were being drained, either for agriculture, or as part of works such as hydroelectric power schemes which ultimately raised the water level, so that nothing is now visible.

We have some evidence from documentary sources for Celtic religious beliefs. They seem to have worshipped a large number of deities identified with natural features such as rivers and woods. One of the most striking survivals is a wooden figure from Ballachulish (1.21), dated to *c*.700–500 BC (Fig. 2). A rough female figure carved from oak, she has quartz eyes. Discovered accidentally by workmen in 1880, surrounded by what may have been a wickerwork shrine, she is now a key exhibit in the Museum of Scotland. 'Archaeology can give only a fragmentary reflection of prehistoric religious life. The

Fig. 2. The 'Ballachulish goddess' (from the original report of the discovery in Proceedings of the Society of Antiquaries of Scotland*) (1.21).*

exceptional survival of the wooden idol from Ballachulish serves to show how much Iron Age religious symbolism was invested in long-vanished perishable materials, while the later Irish texts provide a flavour of the myths, songs, stories and legends that we have lost' (Ian Armit).

Around 200 BC to AD 80 'Celtic' society, language and art forms seem to have been adopted from Europe. This was now a stable society with undefended settlements, normally consisting of groups of round huts. The elite was less warlike, and power seems to have been based on agricultural production. But society was probably still tribal, with occasional intertribal warfare. Gradually larger tribal groupings seem to emerge, with the Picts apparently in charge of much of eastern and northern Scotland. Towards the end of the Iron Age, around AD 500, an increasing number of buildings were rectangular rather than circular. Circular buildings lasted longest in the north and west.

2. PICTS, SCOTS, NORSE AND EARLY CHRISTIANS

The Picts are known about from the mid sixth century AD to the ninth. They were an agricultural society, and our main evidence for their culture is the surviving stones carved with distinctive symbols. The earlier stones are rough boulders, the later ones shaped slabs, incorporating Christian images as well as traditional Pictish ones. In Lochaber, tradition states that the Picts ruled the area north and east of Ardnamurchan. However, Pictish carved stones survive on Skye and Raasay, but not in Lochaber. There was said to have been a Pictish fortress in the area of, or on the site of, Inverlochy Castle. Hector Boece in his *History of Scotland*, published in 1527, refers to King Eoghan II in the ninth century building a great citadel 'to which came many foreign merchants and emissaries' from all the known world.

In about AD 500 the Scots of Antrim (north-east Ireland) moved to a new kingdom of Dalriada, which by the seventh century stretched from Kintyre to Ardnamurchan. Argyll (the name means the coastland of the Gael) was the heart of the kingdom of Dalriada, with its capital at Dunadd. The nearest identified Dalriadan power centre to Lochaber is at Dunollie, just outside Oban. Ardnamurchan Point seems to have been a natural dividing line between Dalriada and Pictdom. In both Pictland and Argyll land seems to have been divided up into large units, subdivided into estates. These units were used for administrative purposes, and for assessment of feudal service. Many boundaries established at this time (or perhaps earlier) have survived to the present day in parish and other administrative, estate and farm boundaries.

The Christian missionary St Ninian, based at Whithorn in the far south-west of Scotland, lived in the fifth century. For the northern parts of Dalriada, however, Christianity was probably not introduced before the arrival of St Columba (521–97) in 563. He first came to an unidentified island in southern Argyll, but later founded a monastery at Iona, which rapidly became established as the most important religious site in Argyll, and a major centre of learning and pilgrimage. The place name element 'Kil' or 'Cille' suggests a possible Celtic Christian origin. Such names are numerous in Lochaber, for example Kilfinnan, Kilmonivaig, and Kilmallie, and may indicate an area of Dalriadan expansion into Pictish territory. They almost certainly imply a religious site dating to between 500 and 900. Some associations with the names of early saints almost certainly imply antiquity. St Maelrubha of Applecross (642–722), St Moluag (523–92), who established a community on Lismore before the founding of the community on Iona, and St Donan were early saints who went out of fashion later, so the survival of their names is likely to be genuine evidence of an early Christian site. However some saints, such as Columba, retained their popularity for a long time, and their names may not necessarily indicate an early association. The name 'Annat' seems to imply an early Christian site, often referring to an earlier site near a medieval one, as at Corpach, to the west of the parish church of Kilmallie. There are another three Annats in Lochaber. There was often continuity between pagan religious sites and Christian ones.

The Picts seem to have encountered Christianity by about 600, but there is little firm evidence until King Nechtan introduced the Roman form of Christianity in the early eighth century. The Roman Church was not based on monasticism but on a hierarchy of bishops and clergy each with authority over a fixed territory. This allowed greater political control. There were also differences such as how the date of Easter was calculated, and the style of tonsure worn by monks. At the Synod of Whitby in 664 the Roman system was chosen in favour of the 'Columban' one, and church and state were to remain closely linked for centuries to come. Although the Picts seem gradually to have become more cohesive politically, their core territory was on the east coast, and their hold on parts of Lochaber may often have been tenuous. There is certainly little surviving physical evidence for their presence. However, the rim of a Pictish bronze hanging bowl, found at Castle Tioram, can be seen in the West Highland Museum in Fort William.

By the seventh century the Christian church was well established among Scots and Picts alike. By the eighth century there was a network of monasteries, which were centres of intellectual and artistic life. The great free-standing crosses on Iona date from the eighth and ninth centuries. The Pictish stone-carvers now added Christian motifs to their traditional designs, and also hunting scenes, animals and fish. Monasteries, with their wealth and international links, were also centres of farming expertise. Lochaber contained no major monastic sites itself, though there were two important centres nearby, at Lismore and Iona. Surviving early Christian monuments include simple crosses on grave markers (like those found at Killundine, Morvern, 3.18) and boundary stones (as at Crois Bheinn, Morvern, 3.9.), but these cannot be closely dated. As with previous periods, evidence in Lochaber is slight, particularly in contrast with the Western Isles and the rest of Argyll. As in Ireland, early churches often sat within circular or sub-circular enclosures, and a few such enclosures can be found in Lochaber, though they may not always be old, and may simply be dictated by topography.

Towards the end of the eighth century, Scotland was disrupted by Viking raids (the first recorded one was in 793). They came by sea, first as raiders, but soon as colonisers. They sailed from Norway to Shetland and Orkney, where they quickly took over control, and from where they gradually expanded south and west. Meanwhile Vikings from Denmark raided the east coasts of Scotland and England. It is not clear why Danish and Norse seafarers chose this period to extend their empire, but it may simply have been that an increase in population created pressure for expansion. Theirs was not an empire in any organised sense, but groups of individuals who were farmers and seafarers, seeking new lands to raid and to settle. They were clearly competent sailors and navigators, and had developed a range of ships, from fine-lined oared sailing warships to tubbier sailing merchant ships. But although Vikings seem to have settled around much of the Scottish coast, they do not appear to have established any urban centre comparable with Dublin in Ireland or York in England.

As they settled they brought their distinctive culture, though it is not clear how far they intermingled with those already living in Scotland. Initially they were pagan, and their burials contain distinctive grave goods. But after about 950 they seem to have adopted Christianity. They lived in long rectangular houses, in contrast to the mainly circular houses of earlier inhabitants. There were certainly Vikings in the west Highlands, as they are known to have sacked Iona four times between 795 and 826. Little evidence of their settlement survives, however, apart from place names. Examples include 'wick', meaning bay; '-dalr', meaning valley (for example Mungasdail, in Morvern); '-bolstadr', meaning farm, which is found in word endings such as 'pool' (for example Ullapool), and '-bo'; and '-nes', meaning headland. 'Tarbet' often signifies a place where boats could be dragged a short distance overland between two expanses of water, as for example between Tarbet on Loch Nevis and Loch Morar. 'Oronsay' means tidal island, and there is an Oronsay off the west end of Morvern. 'Borg' means fort, and while not nearly as common as the Gaelic word 'don', there are some places with this name element, such as Borve and Borrodale. Viking culture was maritime, and the first settlements were often on defended headlands or islands, as bases for further raids. Place names of mixed Norse and Gaelic origin can be found from Morvern up to Knoydart, and in the Ballachulish area, but nowhere east or north of Fort William.

Viking burials come in a variety of forms, some on Pictish burial sites. Most are inhumations, and contain grave goods reflecting the status of the dead person. Many west coast Viking finds were made in the nineteenth century, when archaeology was in its infancy, and give us little information. Most were chance finds, mainly graves, and particularly on islands. There is also evidence for the land divisions they used, probably for tax purposes. 'Ouncelands' can be traced in a number of places including Ardgour and Sunart, and survive in place names and quite possibly in modern land boundaries. Ouncelands were divided into pennylands, but the number of pennylands to an ounceland seems to have varied. This may relate to different administrative systems within the Viking world, or to pre-Viking administrative systems.

In about 843, Kenneth MacAlpin, king of the Scots, defeated or took over the Picts, and became the first king of a united Scotland, which gradually came to be know as Alba. But it was not the whole of modern Scotland, or even the whole of the mainland, as parts of the north and west were controlled by the Norse. The centre of the new kingdom was inevitably in the east, as that is where the best agricultural land is found. But until 1097 Scottish kings continued to be buried on Iona. Although the monastery there was abandoned in 807 after Viking raids, the site retained its importance in memory and tradition.

Ardnamurchan Point is the division between the northern and southern Hebrides, and has for long been a political division. During the twelfth century Somerled ruled Argyll and the southern Hebrides, while the Vikings ruled the western Highlands. The Scots had come over from Ireland, but links between Scotland and Ireland weakened as the Scots became firmly established and intermarried. Somerled, of mixed Norwegian/Celtic background, who had married a Norse princess in 1140, defeated the Norwegian king of the Isle of Man, and in 1156–8 set up his own empire in the Western Isles and western mainland. He had driven the Norsemen out of Lochaber, and in 1156 won a decisive sea battle off Islay. He claimed to be king of Morvern, Lochaber, Argyll and the southern Hebrides. He died fighting King Malcolm's army in 1164. The Norsemen were finally defeated by Alexander III in 1263 at the Battle of Largs.

3. MEDIEVAL AND LATER HISTORY

The Lords of the Isles

In 1229 Alexander II granted to Walter Comyn the extensive lands of Badenoch and Lochaber. The Comyns built castles to defend their new lands, including Inverlochy (Plate 9; Fig. 3). Somerled's 'kingdom' was divided between his four sons with parts of Lochaber gong to two of them. Dugald got Lorne, Lismore and Mull; and his descendants, the Macdougall Lords of Lorne, had their main seat at Dunstaffnage, just north of Oban; Ranald's territories centred on Islay and Kintyre, and the inner Hebrides, but also included Morvern, Ardnamurchan and Moidart. It is his descendants who became the 'Lords of the Isles'. Ranald's younger son Donald was the founder of Clan Donald, and his younger brother Roderick (Ruari) of the MacRuaris of Moidart and Knoydart. The descendants of Somerled built a chain of castles in the thirteenth century along the coasts of Lochaber, including Ardtornish (Figs 4 and 26), Mingary (Fig. 28) and Tioram (Plate 10; Fig. 29). By the later thirteenth century other clans emerged, including the Macleans in Mull and Morvern. The fourteenth century saw improvements to some castles, including Tioram.

The title 'Lord of the Isles' was first used by John MacDonald of Islay, a descendant of Somerled, in 1336. It was a title he claimed, not one given to him by the king or anyone else. But it was a statement of ambition, and he and his direct descendants controlled much the same territory as Somerled had once done for the next 150 years. John's father had achieved the gradual ascendancy of the MacDonalds over the MacDougalls with the support of the crown, but John hedged his bets. In 1336 John Balliol confirmed him in lands covering much

Fig. 3. Inverlochy Castle from the north-west (from MacGibbon & Ross, Castellated and Domestic Architecture*)*

of Argyll, and the southern islands including Mull. This grant was confirmed by David II. In 1346 his first wife inherited lands on the coast between Morvern and Knoydart, and the Uists. A second marriage brought more of southern Argyll, including Kintyre. By the fourteenth century the Camerons, vassals of the MacDonalds, were emerging as a clan, fighting the Mackintoshes over land around Glen Loy and Loch Arkaig. Another emerging clan was the Stewarts of Appin. But all were subordinate to the Lords of the Isles.

Although Scotland had been one country for some time, by the late fourteenth century there was developing the view of a country divided into two parts, the 'civilised' Scots-speaking Lowlanders and the 'savage and untamed' Gaelic-speaking Highlanders, often referred to as 'Irish'. The boundary between the two areas was ill-defined, depending of the agenda of the commentator, and the clan system was not really very different from the feudal system in the rest of Scotland. But within the wild Highlands the crown found it hard to exert control other than through the loyalty of some clans. Too much was happening in the Lowlands, and the king had to rely on the leading landowners to exercise control on his behalf. The Lords of the Isles controlled a large area, and wielded great power.

The Lords of the Isles were patrons of Gaelic culture. They were also patrons of the church, and feudal superiors of all the religious

Fig. 4. Ardtornish Castle from the west (from MacGibbon & Ross, Castellated and Domestic Architecture*)*

houses in the area, including Iona, and of other clans and their chiefs, including the Macleans of Duart, and the Mackintoshes of Glen Loy and Loch Arkaig. John, first Lord of the Isles, died in around 1386 at his castle of Ardtornish and was buried on Iona. Ronald got the northern mainland territories, and founded the Clanranald MacDonalds; Alexander got the eastern part of Lochaber, and founded the Keppoch MacDonalds. Godfrey was given the Uists, and John Mor parts of Kintyre and Islay. Donald was his main heir. John Mor rebelled, but was defeated, retreated to Ireland, married there and established the MacDonalds of Antrim.

There was little possibility of expanding MacDonald lands north or east without coming into conflict with other great landowners. From 1398 to 1415 Donald was in dispute with the duke of Albany over the earldom of Ross and lordship of Skye. The two main castles of the Lordship were Aros on Mull and Ardtornish on Morvern (Figs 4 and 26), from where there was easy access to the mainland and the Great Glen. Donald was succeeded in about 1423 by his son Alexander, who fell out with James I. He was arrested, but released after a few years. Bitter after this experience, Alexander launched attacks on the borders of his lands. In 1429 he burned Inverness. But this provoked a response in force, and late that year a royal army defeated him in Lochaber. But the conflict still simmered, and in

January 1431 James and his army were defeated at Inverlochy. In 1431 there was a public reconciliation, and in 1436 Alexander was recognised as earl of Ross. With the title came lands beyond the Highlands, which subsequently took much of his attention. As a result of this the minor branches of the MacDonalds, such as the Clanranalds, gained increased power within their own territories. The Macleods gained a firmer hold on Skye, and the Mackintoshes in Lochaber. When Alexander died in 1449 he was buried in the cathedral at Fortrose, in Easter Ross.

His son John was about fifteen when he succeeded. He made several political miscalculations, and spent his first few years fighting to retain his eastern lands. His relationship with James II was bad, and with James III worse. Edward IV of England saw him as a potential ally, and in 1462 he and John signed the Treaty of Westminster-Ardtornish, agreeing to divide up a conquered Scotland, though nothing came of this grandiose plan. However, fourteen years later, when the Scottish king found out about it, he deprived John of his lands. Eventually he was allowed to retain the core Lordship lands, and the title, but lost the lands and offices he had held in Inverness and Easter Ross. Back in his heartlands, he had to deal with his relatives who had extended their power base while his attentions had been engaged elsewhere. There was virtual civil war in the area, culminating in the Battle of Bloody Bay, at the north end of Mull, where John's fleet was defeated by one led by his son Angus Og, who thereby became de facto Lord of the Isles.

The Crown gradually gained the support of the Campbells in southern Argyll, and the Mackintoshes further north. Angus Og continued rebelling against the crown, and trying to recover his lands in Ross. In 1490, however, when he was well on the way to achieving this, he was assassinated. The Campbells captured his son and heir and imprisoned him. John became Lord of the Isles again, but in a very weak position. In 1493 James IV decreed that his lands and Lordship were forfeit. John died in obscurity ten years later in Dundee. But it was only with the death of his grandson

Donald in 1545 that the MacDonalds finally lost their control over much of the western Highlands and islands. Their pre-eminent position was taken over by the Campbells, who controlled much of southern Argyll.

All the clans who were once vassals of the Lords of the Isles now held their lands directly from the Crown. Clan Maclean held Mull, Coll, Tiree, Kingairloch, Morvern and Ardgour. After the forfeiture of the Lordship of the Isles, the clan split into four groups, based at Duart, Lochbuie, Coll and Ardgour. Most of the heart of Lochaber, which had belonged first to the Macdougalls of Lorn, then the MacDonalds, became dominated after their forfeiture by the Camerons. Moidart, Arisaig, Morar and Knoydart were also MacDonald lands, while Ardnamurchan belonged to an offshoot of the MacDonalds, the MacIans (ousted by the Campbells in 1625). There were various battles or skirmishes between local clans. At Dun Dige, for example, in Glen Nevis, MacSorlies were massacred by Mackintoshes in 1495. The Mackintoshes moved east to Badenoch, and some of their lands were taken over by the Camerons, but without legal title, causing many later disputes. Clan Cameron consisted of four branches, the MacMartins of Letterfinlay, the Camerons of Locheil, the MacGillonies of Strone and the MacSorlies of Glen Nevis.

James IV learned Gaelic, and took the trouble to visit the Highlands to socialise with the clan chiefs. He was also interested in gunnery, and built up his navy. Henry VIII of England became ambitious to regain lands in France, causing problems for James, who had alliances with both England and France. When Henry invaded France in 1513, James felt compelled to invade England in support of the French. But he did not get far, and was defeated and killed at the Battle of Flodden.

John Macculloch, in 1824, wrote that 'In the maritime Highlands, as might be expected, the castles are generally situated near the margins of the water; and often, apparently, rather for the convenience of embarkation than from notions of defence'. But while the original situation of these castles was very often maritime, ensuring control of the seaways, this centuries-old tradition came to an end with the introduction of armed warships. In 1540 James V mounted an expedition to the Highlands and Islands, to demonstrate royal control of the area. The development of seaborne artillery meant that castles could be bombarded effectively from the sea, and thus central government found itself at last able to exert effective control over areas which for long had enjoyed a great degree of autonomy. James's attempts to win over the MacDonalds, however, were unsuccessful. When Henry VIII invaded Scotland in 1542, he was supported by many Highlanders, including the Macleans of Ardgour, and the MacDonalds of Clanranald and Ardnamurchan, who attacked the lands of the Campbells of Argyll, who were loyal to the Scottish crown. But the Highland effort soon collapsed in acrimony. The Scots counter-attack was routed at Solway Moss, and James died soon afterwards.

Despite armed warships, however, royal power remained distant and difficult to enforce, and in this power vacuum clan feuding continued. The Battle of the Shirts, fought near Laggan in 1544 (11.3), was the largest inter-clan battle ever fought, with the Frasers fighting a coalition of MacDonalds, Macdonnells and Camerons. As explained by Samuel Johnson

> the inhabitants of mountains form distinct races, and are careful to preserve their genealogies. Men in a small district necessarily mingle blood by intermarriages, and combine at last into one family, with a common interest in the honour and disgrace of every individual. Then begins that union of affections, and co-operation of endeavours, that constitute a clan . . . Thus every Highlander can talk of his ancestors, and recount the outrages which they suffered from the wicked inhabitants of the next valley. Such are the effects of habitation among mountains . . .

Clan warfare was endemic, and as the clans feuded, their relative fortunes changed. Johnson commented how the chiefs still had great independence, dispensing their own justice, and at a great distance

Fig. 5. Free-standing cross, Kiel, Morvern

from central government. 'A claim of lands between two powerful lairds was decided like a contest for dominion between sovereign powers. They drew their forces into the field, and right attended on the strongest. This was, in ruder times, the common practice, which the kings of Scotland could seldom control'. A frequent source of dispute was cattle raiding. As Thomas Pennant put it in 1769 'Lochaber had been a den of thieves; and as long as they had their waters, their torrents and their bogs, in a state of nature, they made their excursions, could plunder and retreat with their booty in full security.' The law was too weak to do anything. 'A contribution, called the *Black-meal*, was raised by several of these plundering chieftains over a vast extent of country; whoever payed it had their cattle ensured, but those who dared to refuse were sure to suffer.'

A distinctive culture developed in the area, demonstrated by the medieval sculpture which survives in some of the many burial grounds.

This art form was possibly introduced, and certainly encouraged to flourish, by the Lords of the Isles, and was ended by the Reformation. These striking monuments can be attributed to various schools of stone carving within the area of Argyll and the Western Isles, of which the Iona workshop may have been the earliest. Examples of its work, both a free-standing cross and decorated grave slabs, can be seen at Kiel church, at Lochaline, in Morvern (3.3) (Plates 3, 4, 6; Fig. 5). There are also carved stones at Kilchoan, in Ardnamurchan (3.16.), and at Arisaig (3.20). Most of the late medieval carved stones are found in churches on or near the coast, because of the difficulties of overland transport.

The main events of the mid sixteenth century, associated with the Reformation, had little impact on the Highlands. James VI tried hard to exercise real control. In 1597, for example, he demanded that all Highland landowners had to produce their title deeds, and give a promise of loyalty and good behaviour. He tried, as had been done in Ulster, to settle Lowlanders and even Englishmen in the Highlands, to set an example of improved agriculture and administration. He planned a plantation in Lochaber, but it did not happen. The settlers in Lewis were driven away by local hostility, and only in Kintyre did he have partial success. The king also enlisted the help of those families who were willing, to act as his agents. The families who conformed, such as the Campbells, did well by comparison with those families, such as the Macleans, who refused to sacrifice their traditional independence. Clan MacGregor was completely proscribed.

But by the end of the century, with the Highlands still barely under royal control, James VI succeeded to the throne of England, and he and his court moved south. Only a few of the richest aristocrats could afford to remain involved in a Parliament sitting in London, and the Highlands were now a very long way from the heart of government. The main country-wide administrative organisation was the church. In 1616 the Privy Council decreed that there should be a school in every parish, and in 1633, and again in 1646, that the heritors (property owners) should provide the money. But with such vast parishes in the Highlands, even where schools were set up they only in practical terms served a fraction of the children who might have benefited from them. The care of the poor was also a parish responsibility. Outwith burghs – of which there was none in Lochaber until the founding of Gordonsburgh (later renamed Fort William) in 1618 – the only administrative body was the church.

The seventeenth century was a troubled period in the history of this area, with issues of loyalty to the crown, differences of religious belief, and inter-clan disputes intertwined to create an ever-changing pattern of alliances and hostilities. In 1644 Alastair MacColla, Montrose's second-in-command, bringing troops from Ireland, attacked Kinlochaline Castle on Morvern, and then Mingary Castle on Ardnamurchan (Fig. 28). Montrose's forces campaigned over the winter of 1644–5, defeating the Campbell earl of Argyll at the battle of Inverlochy (11.4). Later that year Montrose had other victories, culminating in the battle of Kilsyth. But outside the Highlands his support did not grow, and some of his Highland troops went home. He was defeated eventually at Philliphaugh, near Selkirk.

In 1653–4 there was a Royalist rebellion in the Highlands, led by the earl of Glencairn, and supported by the Mackenzies, Camerons, Macleans, MacDonalds of Keppoch and Macdonnells of Glengarry. But it was ineffective. As a result, however, in 1654 General Monk built the first fort at what was later to become Fort William (7.1), as well as forts at Inverness, Leith, Perth and Stirling. Sir Ewan Cameron of Locheil led local guerrilla opposition to the garrison at Inverlochy for the first year, before agreeing terms. Some castles experienced a final, and humiliating, use as subsidiary government garrisons during the various disturbances of the seventeenth century.

The Jacobites

James II gradually strengthened royal powers and was becoming increasingly pro-Catholic. His second wife was a Roman Catholic, and when a son was born in 1688 a crisis was precipitated. James's

Fig. 6. A Highland ring-brooch, found on the wreck of HMS Dartmouth

daughter Mary and her husband, Prince William of Orange, were invited to come to Britain as Protestant and constitutional monarchs (the 'Glorious Revolution'). William of Orange landed in south-west England in 1689, and opposition in the Highlands was led by John Graham of Claverhouse, 'Bonnie Dundee', who defeated William's army at the battle of Killiecrankie, but died of his wounds. Once again the Highland clan chiefs were invited to sign an oath of loyalty, and three naval vessels were sent to back up the threat, including HMS *Dartmouth*, which was wrecked in the Sound of Mull (Fig. 6). Tradition has it that her wrecking was the work of the Mull witches, who naturally took the side of the Jacobite Macleans of Duart.

The government of William and Mary wanted to secure the future loyalty of those who had supported the deposed James VII, among whom were the MacDonalds of Glencoe. In 1691 a pardon was offered to all those who had opposed the new government, provided they swore an oath of allegiance before a sheriff before 1 January 1692. But on the assumption that submission would not be total, the government at the same time made plans for punitive action. MacIan of Glencoe went to the commander of the garrison at Fort William to sign the oath, only to be told that he was not the right person, and he had to go to the sheriff at Inveraray. There was no time to get there before the deadline, but MacIan set off anyway. When he got to Inveraray the sheriff was not there, and it was 6 January before the oath was signed.

Communications between Edinburgh, Inveraray and Fort William were slow, and before MacIan appeared it was decided to make an example of Glencoe. Instructions were sent to the troops based in Fort William. In February soldiers were billeted in the glen, and on 12 February more troops were ordered there, with instructions to 'fall upon the rebels, the McDonalds of Glencoe, and put all to the sword under seventy'. Out of an estimated population of 150, about 38 were killed, and many houses burned and livestock driven away, so it is thought that many more died afterwards of exposure or wounds while hiding from the troops. Many people were shocked, and questions were asked. In 1695 an enquiry was ordered. It concluded that there had been no justification for such brutality, that the soldiers had exceeded their orders, but the blame did not go to the highest level. Colonel Hill, however, the governor of the garrison at Fort William, ensured that the survivors were resettled in the glen.

From 1688 onwards, Lochaber had been at the centre of support for the exiled James VII and later his son and grandson. This support was partly natural conservatism, partly political and partly religious. James had been a Roman Catholic, while most of England was Church of England, and most Scots were Presbyterian. Politically the Stuarts had believed in the divine right of kings, and had resented the growing power of Parliament. William and Mary had been invited to take over, on strict terms, as the first constitutional monarchs. Not everyone found this easy to accept, feeling that the rightful king, however flawed, should be supported. The divine right of kings perhaps made more sense to those used to the clan system than those outside it.

The Jacobites were not an organised movement in the modern sense. There was very little co-ordination between the various groups based in Scotland, Ireland and England. Many Scottish Jacobites belonged to the Episcopal rather than the Roman Catholic church. There were even a few Presbyterians who joined out of clan loyalty. In Ireland, Jacobitism was related to nationalism, which was also an expression of the Catholic majority against English Protestant minority rule. In England the movement appealed to Catholics and to conservatives who could not accept the Glorious Revolution. The core of support in Scotland lay in the Highlands, within the clan system, though not all clans were Jacobite. And as time went on support dwindled.

The government enacted measures to gain more control over the Highlands. In 1695 they passed an Act setting up 'English Schools for rooting out the Irish [Gaelic] language and other pious uses'. 1707 saw the Act of Union, by which Scotland, albeit perhaps reluctantly, agreed to political union with England. But when Queen Anne died in 1714, with no surviving children, a crisis was precipitated. Her brother James Edward Stuart ('The Old Pretender', 1688–1766) was a Catholic, and so banned from the throne, which therefore passed to a German cousin, of the house of Hanover, who became George I. He was very far from being the nearest in line, but all those with a stronger claim to the throne were Roman Catholics. To many people, however, the rejection of Stuart heirs in favour of someone so distant and foreign was unreasonable. At first, however, some of the leading Jacobites tried to work with King George, and it was only a year after his succession, when the earl of Mar quarrelled with the king, that rebellion was planned.

The 1715 rising

Although Mar had the support of the MacDonalds, Camerons and Mackintoshes, much of the action in 1715 took place in the eastern Highlands. Mar was not a good leader. The rebel standard was raised at Braemar, and progress checked by Argyll at the indecisive battle of Sheriffmuir. The Old Pretender, the son of James VII, landed at Peterhead, and the Jacobites marched south, but were defeated at Preston. James, who also proved not a very successful leader, had already fled back to France.

In the aftermath of this rebellion, those most closely involved had their estates confiscated, and the clans were forbidden to carry arms. General Wade was sent to take control of the Highlands, which he saw meant building roads to supply the forts he was to build, and to allow troops to move around faster if needed. At the same time loyal Highlanders were recruited into the British army.

The Forty-Five

There was an abortive rising in 1719, with the help of Spanish troops. In 1739 Britain declared war on France, and the Jacobites hoped for French support for their cause. But the French were lukewarm, and it was 1744 before there was an attempted French-backed invasion across the English Channel. But it was thwarted by a gale, and there was to be no further support from France. During the winter of 1744–5 Jacobite agents tried to assess the degree of support they might gain. It was less than they might have hoped, but a decision to abandon the planned rising was overtaken by events, as a result of a failure of communication. The Young Pretender, Charles Edward Stuart (1720–88), set off from France in two ships, but the one carrying most of the weapons was intercepted by a British ship off the Lizard, and the other vessel sailed on alone.

The Prince landed on Eriskay, using a pilot picked up on Barra, and soon sailed on to Loch nan Uamh, landing on the north shore at the mouth of the Borrodale Burn, near Arisaig House (12.3). Visitors to the ship included the poet Alexander MacDonald. The Prince came ashore on 11 August, and set off with the 'seven men of Moidart' (12.4). These were Aeneas MacDonald, a banker in Paris, and the only local, being the brother of the laird of Kinlochmoidart; William Murray, Marquis of Tullibardine; Sir John MacDonald, who served in the French army; Francis Strickland, an English supporter; Sir

Thomas Sheridan, the Prince's old tutor; George Kelly, a clergyman; and John William O'Sullivan, an Irish mercenary. Most of them were elderly.

The standard was raised at Glenfinnan (12.5), at the head of Loch Shiel, on 19 August. Many of the clan chiefs were half-hearted in their support, and at first the Prince was only joined by 150 MacDonalds. After a few hours, however, more men arrived, including 700 Camerons led by Locheil, and 300 Keppoch MacDonalds. The first skirmish was at High Bridge (11.6) (Plate 13), at the foot of Glen Spean. The rebels marched east to Speyside, then south to Perth, arriving on 4 September, where new supporters joined them, including Lord George Murray, the younger brother of the duke of Atholl. They continued southward to capture Edinburgh (though not the castle) and routed government troops under Sir John Cope at Prestonpans on 20 September. Many British soldiers were serving abroad, and the numbers available in Scotland were not great.

After a brief rest, with the court established at Holyrood, the Jacobite army left Edinburgh on 1 November and marched into England. They expected more men to rally to the cause, but few did. On 4 December they reached Derby, close to where the duke of Cumberland's army was waiting. However, despite panic in London, the lack of support caused the Jacobites to retreat back into Scotland. On 17 January 1746 they won another battle at Falkirk, but still retreated towards the heartland of their support further north. At Culloden, outside Inverness, short of men and money, and confused about tactics, they faced well-organised government troops. The battle was muddled and short, and ended in total defeat. The wounded and prisoners were harshly treated, because the rebellion had seriously frightened the government.

The Prince fled to near Fort Augustus, then to Invergarry. Soon afterwards he received a letter of resignation from Lord George Murray. He moved west via Loch Arkaig and Arisaig to Benbecula, then Lewis, then Skye, then back to the mainland, moving around to avoid capture. On 15 August 1746 he was at Loch Arkaig, and on

19 September he left Scotland for ever from Loch nan Uamh on a French ship.

In the aftermath of Culloden, a few of the ringleaders were executed, while others had their estates confiscated, and throughout the Highlands lairds' houses were burned. Acts were passed banning the carrying of weapons without express permission, and the wearing of Highland dress. Also abolished were 'heritable jurisdictions' – the rights of landowners to dispense minor justice themselves. This greatly enhanced the control of central government over the administration of justice in remote areas.

The last of the punitive demonstrations of government power was in Appin, near Ballachulish. James Stewart of the Glen was tried and executed in 1752 (12.6). Accused of being an accessory to the assassination of Colin Campbell of Glenure, who was an agent for the forfeited estates, Stewart was framed so that someone could be made an example of to remind the Jacobites of Lochaber of the power of the Hanoverian government.

As well as the garrison at Fort William, a small body of troops was stationed for several years at the west end of Loch Arkaig (Tigh nan Saighdearan, NM 981 914: OS 40). These measures marked the end of the old clan system, and very soon the Highlands were a valued part of Britain, providing troops to fight in the many wars. Highland landowners gradually lost their regional differences and idiosyncrasies. In the 1780s the punitive legislation was repealed, and the forfeited estates returned to their owners. Highlanders were serving loyally in the British army, and the Highlands were both economically and socially becoming part of mainstream society.

The history of the area from the later eighteenth century, therefore, is dealt with in subsequent sections on a thematic basis.

4. THE CHURCH

Christianity was brought to Lochaber in the sixth century, from areas to the south and west. Early Christian sites can often be identified by the place name 'Kil', meaning cell or church, and the names of early saints such as St Columba (Colm), St Donan, St Finan, and St Moluag (as in Kilmonivaig). Although there are a number of early church sites in Lochaber, there seem to have been no major monastic sites. The nearest medieval monasteries were a Benedictine abbey and an Augustinian nunnery on Iona, and a Valliscaulian house at Ardchattan, founded c.1230 by Duncan Macdougall of Lorne. In the other direction were the Dominican house at Inverness and the Carmelite friary at Kingussie. There were some monks in the twelfth century at Arisaig, but otherwise nothing within Lochaber. Lochaber lay within the medieval diocese of Argyll, with its administrative centre on Lismore. Turf walls near Kiel church, in Morvern, are known as 'the bishop's house' (NM 667 454: OS 49). This seems to relate to Hector Maclean, minister of Morvern from 1639 to 1679, and also tacksman of Kiel, who was appointed bishop of Argyll in 1680. To the north, the diocese of the Highlands had its cathedral sites in the more populated part of the region, as for example at Dornoch.

By the twelfth century a parochial system for church administration had been established. 'The Highlands, before the Reformation, was well provided both in churches and clergymen . . . as well as the numerous vestiges of small religious houses, which every traveller perceived . . .' Parish churches in this area in c.1300 included Arisaig, Eilean Fhianain (Loch Shiel), Eilean Munde (Loch Leven), Kilchoan (Ardnamurchan), Kilchoan (Inverie, Knoydart),

Cill Choluimchille (Kiel, Morvern), Killintag (Fernish, Morvern), Kilmallie, Kilmonivaig and Moidart. The medieval churches were very simple buildings, and all that survives of them are fragments in graveyards or incorporated into the fabric of later churches. 'Since the reformation, many buildings have been erased, and the materials applied to other purposes; some are mouldering away with time, and the number of parishes has been greatly contracted' (Knox, 1786).

A distinctive feature of this area is its burial isles. It is said that the Gaels believed that for souls to reach Tir nan Og their bodies had to cross water before burial. There may also have been more practical reasons for keeping burial sites separate from domestic sites. The elite were buried on Iona, and both Corpach and Onich were places where bodies were embarked to be taken for burial on Iona. But other people were buried on islands closer to where they had lived, such as Eilean Munde in Loch Leven (Plate 11) and Eilean Fhianain on Loch Shiel. Ancient coffin roads lead towards these islands from a wide area, often with resting cairns along the route, to which a stone was added for each passing coffin.

> The Reformation came and went
> with fighting and with storming:
> The Highland clans paid little heed,
> For they were past reforming.

In the early seventeenth century, because of a lack of ministers, several parishes were merged, but this did not help as, even if a minister could be found, the areas were too large to be worked effectively. Kilchoan, Eilean Fhianain and Kilmory were merged to create the vast parish of Ardnamurchan, and the two parts of Morvern were joined together. Changes to the established church did not help either. After the Restoration Charles II restored Episcopal rule to the church. This was abolished again in 1689, and Presbyterian government restored in 1690. Some ministers agreed to accept the changes, but some with Episcopal sympathies chose to leave or were forced out by the general assembly. These included nationally more than two-thirds of those in post, and locally the ministers of Ardnamurchan and Morvern. It took time, however, and some Episcopalian ministers survived for several years until replacements could be found.

The new Highland parishes were enormous. Kilmallie, for example, is 60 miles long, and 30 miles at its widest, containing about 400,000 acres (Kilmonivaig was 300,000 acres, Ardnamurchan 200,000 acres, Morvern a mere 65,000 acres). To complicate matters, parts of Kilmallie and of Ardnamurchan were in Inverness-shire and parts in Argyll. And the difficult terrain made the work of the parish priest or minister even harder. 'The fatigues and inconveniences to the clergy, in the discharge of their duty . . . cannot be conceived by those who have not seen these countries' (Knox, 1786). Not only was the area to be covered impossibly large, but stipends were poor. Knox reported they averaged £50 per annum, compared with £80 in the Lowlands. Missionaries were introduced, but as they were paid even less than trained ministers and had to contend with similar problems, their numbers and effectiveness were not very great. By contrast, Knox claimed, the Roman Catholic clergy had churches and houses 'in excellent repair'. Some areas were hardly covered by the kirk. There is a Gaelic saying that 'There was never a minister's sermon in Blessed Morar, until the railway came'.

By the eighteenth century many parish churches were in disrepair. The *Old Statistical Account* provides a picture of the situation in the 1790s. The minister of Kilmonivaig had no manse or glebe. In Kilmallie there were nine places of worship, to be served by one minister, plus a missionary in Fort William, and extra people were sometimes employed. A new parish church had been built in 1783, with another provided for Maryburgh (Fort William) in 1791 by the duke of Gordon. But there was a dispute over patronage between the duke and Cameron of Locheil.

No early post-Reformation churches survive, if any were indeed built. By 1642 all churches were required to have a bell, though most were hung in simple bellcotes, as few Highland rural churches have towers. In general terms, the medieval buildings suffered neglect, and were not very big, so when they were replaced it was often on a different site. It would have been hard to build a new larger church within the confines of the old graveyard without enormous disruption, so most post-Reformation churches were built on new sites. Clearly much depended on the availability of land, but sometimes the new church was adjacent to the old one, as at Kiel, Morvern, and sometimes on a new site, perhaps to be more accessible to the new road network, as at Fernish, Morvern. Manses, if provided at all, had also been simple, and were being rebuilt or improved at this period. At Kilmonivaig, for example, a water closet was added in 1804. By the 1830s Morvern had a new manse, but both churches were in a state of disrepair. Many eighteenth-century churches were replaced during the later nineteenth century, and few survive to be visited.

John Carsewell, bishop of the Isles, had translated John Knox's liturgy into Gaelic in the later sixteenth century, and there were various other Gaelic religious publications. However, a complete Bible in Scots Gaelic was not published until 1801. Conscious of the poor state of many Highland churches, the Government in 1823 passed an Act for Building Additional Places of Worship in the Highlands and Islands of Scotland. From 1825 to 1835 it financed the building of thirty new churches and forty-three manses. The engineer Thomas Telford was in charge of the scheme, but most of the churches seem to have been designed by his surveyor William Thomson. The standard design was T-shaped, which seated 312, and cost about £600, but up to three galleries could be added, seating another 60 each. A smaller, cheaper version could be built as a rectangle. These churches were simple but well-built, usually of harled rubble with a slate roof, Tudor-arched windows, and a simple bellcote. They set a standard for others to follow. A total of twenty-one were built in the Highlands and Islands, five of them in Lochaber – at Acharacle (Plate 16), Ardgour, Duror, Onich and Strontian, with surviving manses at Acharacle (Fig. 7), Duror and Onich.

Church building and rebuilding continued throughout the nineteenth century and well into the twentieth as new communities

Fig. 7. Parliamentary Manse, Acharacle (5.1)

grew up and sub-parishes were created. St Columba's parish church at Mallaig was built in 1903; and the parish church at Kinlochleven in 1930. Landowners and others in the congregation also demanded more from their place of worship, in terms of size and status, and by the later nineteenth century in terms of decoration. This period saw the introduction of stained glass windows and other features to embellish what had once been very plain buildings. Even when churches moved to new sites, the traditional graveyards tended to remain in use, providing continuity in a changing world, certainly continuity with the medieval church, but quite possibly back into pre-Christian times. The minister of Morvern in the 1830s described how, near both his churches, 'is a church-yard, or burying-ground, but now without any fence, though anciently their precincts were distinctly marked, and considered as sanctuaries'.

Catholicism in the West Highlands was a relic of pre-Reformation days. But as Catholics came increasingly to be persecuted during the seventeenth century, the faith was kept alive in this area by visiting Irish priests and monks. A cross-marked stone in Glen Roy, known as the 'Mass Stone' (3.8), is said to have been used as an altar by Roman Catholic priests during this period of persecution. About two-thirds of Scottish Catholics in the seventeenth and eighteenth centuries were in the Highlands, particularly in Moidart, Arisaig and Morar, along with some of the islands. The church made a concerted attempt during the eighteenth century to minister to its flock, and numbers of both priests and communicants increased. Most Roman Catholic priests were trained in Scots colleges abroad. But by 1714

Fig. 8. Engraving of the 'Floating Church' moored off Strontian (from Brown, Annals of the Disruption)

there was a seminary on Eilean Ban in Loch Morar, specifically to train Gaelic-speaking priests. It moved to Arisaig in 1738, but was abandoned after Culloden. Another opened in Glenfinnan, but soon failed for lack of funds. Training for Gaelic priests was re-established in 1768 at Buorblach, in Morar Bay, but after ten years was transferred to Samalaman, near Glenuig. This in turn closed in 1804, and moved to Lismore, which closed in 1831, merging with Blairs in Kincardineshire. There were three problems in expanding Catholicism. Lack of money, because the local congregations were poor and the central organisation far away; Royalist and Jacobite sympathies; and internal disputes over doctrine.

The early nineteenth century saw evangelical missionaries moving into the area, appealing to poor tenants who saw the ministers as siding with landlords. As a result of this, when the Disruption of the Church of Scotland came in 1843, it had a great effect in the Highlands. Most landowners stayed with the established church, but there were many who joined the Free Church. Nationally about one third of ministers left, but in the Highlands the figure was more than

Fig. 9. 'Preaching at the Sea Side', a frequent scene in the early days after the Disruption (from Brown, Annals of the Disruption*)*

half. At Strontian, where most of the tenants seceded, the landlord, Sir James Riddell, refused their request for land on which to build a church, so a boat was acquired (an enclosed flat-bottomed barge, from the Clyde), at a cost of £1,400 (Fig. 8). The next question was where she should be anchored. 'The best place, safest for the ship, and most convenient for the people, would have been just under the windows of Sir James Riddell's Mansion, but, as a matter of good taste, another was chosen two miles off [in Ardnastang Bay], and there, at a point about 150 yards from the shore, the vessel was safely moored.' It was used for services between 1846 and 1873, when a church was finally built on shore.

At Kilmallie (Corpach), ground was also refused, so the congregation met 'on a little green spot upon the sea-shore, within high-water mark, immediately below the public road, opposite the monument of Colonel John Cameron' (Fig. 9). After a few months a large tent was acquired, and later a wooden shed. The minister had to leave his manse, and ended up living in 'a hut twelve feet square and six feet high, and so open it was necessary by means of blankets and bedcovers to stop out the wind and rain'. Eventually, a patch of boggy ground was given to build a church on. The congregation in Fort William first worshipped in the Craigs Burial Ground. Most early Free Church buildings were similar to Parliamentary churches, simple and relatively cheap. But as the church prospered from the 1860s most were rebuilt more ambitiously. Examples in Lochaber include Spean Bridge (1860), Acharacle (1868), Strontian (1869–73), South Ballachulish (1874), Kilchoan (1876–7), Arisaig (1879–80) and Lochaline (1896).

The nineteenth century also saw almost all established churches rebuilt, sometimes on a third new site, sometimes replacing the eighteenth-century church. It also saw the splitting of the largest parishes, and the building of more churches within existing parishes. In Kilmallie, for example, as well as the parish church at Corpach, there were also churches at Fort William (Duncansburgh), Onich (McIntosh Memorial Church, Nether Lochaber), Kinlochleven, and Achnacarry (Fig. 31). Kingairloch was moved from Lismore and Appin parish to Kilmallie in 1891, and then joined Ardgour when it left Lismore and Appin to become a separate parish in 1895. Arisaig and Moidart was separated from Ardnamurchan in 1895, and Mallaig and Morar from Arisaig and Moidart in 1929. These changes reflected the sheer size of the early parishes, and also the creation of new centres of population, such as Mallaig and Kinlochleven.

Because of the vast size of Highland parishes, and the difficulty of finding ministers willing to work in them, Episcopalian worship and Roman Catholicism both survived in this area. In 1792 the Roman Catholic and Episcopal churches had been freed from legal restrictions on their activities. In the second half of the nineteenth century the Episcopal Church set up its own parochial system, and built new churches, concentrating on centres of population. Examples include St John's, Ballachulish (1842), St Adamnan's, Duror (1848), St Moluag's, Kentallen (1868), St Bride's, North Ballachulish (1874–5) and St Paul's, Kinlochleven (1954). Many were small, recognising that they were mainly to serve the landowner and his household. St

Mary's in Strontian, 'designed and superintended to completion' by Sir Thomas and Lady Riddell of Horseley Hall, was described as 'a very pretty little church, perfect, indeed, for its size, though in the last respect, too, it is probably quite large enough for the requirements of the district'.

Roman Catholic churches were also built where congregations were largest, including Arisaig (1810–11) (Fig. 32), Bunroy (1826), St Mun's, Ballachulish (1836), St Agnes, Glenuig (1861), Our Lady of the Angels, Mingarry (1862) and Our Lady and St Cumin, Morar (1889). This process has continued into the twentieth century, with St Margaret's, Roybridge (1929) (Fig. 37), St Patrick's, Mallaig (1935), St Joseph's, Spean Bridge (1967) and St John's, Corpach (1970). According to the historian and photographer M.E.M. Donaldson, the Catholic Church in the Highlands produced buildings with 'simple dignity', 'utterly devoid of the tawdry trappings which one sees so plentifully even in England'. Some, however, have gone out of use, including St Columba's, Drimnin (1838) and Lochailort (1874).

As a result of all these developments, plus in some cases the desire of landowners to build churches worthy of their status, almost any reasonably sized settlement in the Highlands may now have, as well as an early graveyard, a nineteenth-century Church of Scotland church, a Free Church (perhaps now used as a hall or converted to a house), and often a Roman Catholic and an Episcopal church as well.

In 1581 the Reformed Church forbade the old custom of burial within churches. From the seventeenth century many landed families built burial enclosures within communal graveyards. When church sites moved, graveyards usually stayed put. Although there are some burials around later churches, as for example at the Parliamentary church at Strontian, in most cases the medieval graveyard has remained in use, and modern extensions are attached to the medieval graveyard rather than the more recent church, even where, as in the case at Mungasdail, in Morvern, there is no vehicular access. In some cases, eighteenth- and nineteenth-century burials have covered the ruins of the medieval church. In addition to these communal burial grounds, there are other family or even individual burials dotted around the Highland landscape. Only a few are listed in the Gazetteer, but more are marked on OS maps.

At various places along the traditional coffin routes to churches and particularly to burial isles can be found 'coffin cairns' or 'resting cairns' to which stones were added each time a coffin passed. Some are round-topped, as for example the one at the top of Glencoe, while others are beehive-shaped. According to M.E.M. Donaldson, 'Sometimes, instead of a funeral party being content to add to a common cairn, each will make its own', leading to clusters on some sites. Although the slowly accumulated cairns represent a long tradition, by the nineteenth century some whole cairns were being erected as monuments to individuals. Those by the track up to St Cyril's church in Glen Spean, for example, include monuments to Euan Macdonnell, who was in the Indian Mutiny, and one erected in 1891 to commemorate D. P. MacDonald of the Ben Nevis Distillery. Those beside the road between Loch Shiel and Kinlochmoidart (Plate 17) include one constructed to commemorate General Robertson of Kinlochmoidart, who died in the 1860s.

Schools

The vast size of most Highland parishes meant that many children could not realistically travel to the parish school. The Society in Scotland for Propagating Christian Knowledge (SSPCK), established in 1709, set up schools in areas which needed them, while some farmers shared private tutors. In Knoydart, for example, in the 1790s a school provided by the SSPCK taught thirty to forty children. Kilmallie had a parish school in Fort William, teaching around 150 pupils, and five further ones provided by the SSPCK. Kilmonivaig had a parish school, with twenty to fifty pupils, and two SSPCK schools, but needed two more 'owing to the discontiguity of its several districts'. In Morvern, the parish school, poorly endowed, taught about fifty pupils (including six girls). There was also a SPCK school, and a spinning mistress, 'the benefit of which would be more sensibly felt, were there a method of providing the poorer sort with a few wheels, and some lint'. 'The people are in general industrious, had they a subject to work upon, or a proper stimulus'. And 'besides these public places of education, there are 7 or 8 gentlemen tacksmen who keep private teachers in their families, as they can have no access to the public schools, on account of the distance'.

When county councils were established in the 1880s rural schooling became one of their responsibilities. The first such school in the area was Fort William Senior Secondary School. Some children, however, did go to university, usually Glasgow. In *Reminiscences of a Highland Parish* Norman MacLeod described how in the mid nineteenth century his father had travelled by boat and on foot from Morvern to Glasgow, carrying a bundle containing £20, two shirts and two pairs of socks, a journey which took ten days. He lived frugally in lodgings, and walked back at the end of the academic year.

Few early schools were well housed, many being held in private houses or churches. At Lochaline the little session-house beyond the church was once both schoolhouse and home for the teacher. By the third quarter of the nineteenth century specialised school buildings began to be provided, with high ceilings to increase light and fresh air and reduce the risk of airborne infection. By the end of the nineteenth century there were state-provided schools all over the area. During the twentieth century many of these were closed as the population decreased. After the Second World War junior secondary schools were established at Kinlochleven and Mallaig, and at Tobermory, which took children from Ardnamurchan and Morvern. For the more academic children, there were high schools at Fort William and at Oban, with hostels for children who needed to board during the week.

5. FORT WILLIAM OR
AN GEARASDAN [THE GARRISON]

He who does not know what is the meaning of a 'soft day', must come
to Fort William. (Macculloch, 1824)

According to the *Old Statistical Account* 'There was, at one time, a
thriving borough . . . which some of the old Scotch historians call
the Emporium of the west of Scotland; but of this borough, there
are now no other vestiges, than some paved works in different places,
which were probably the streets of it'. The area around Fort William
is such a logical position for a settlement that it is hard to believe that
there was not something before the present fort and town, but there
is no clear archaeological or historical evidence. There was a strong
local tradition, however, of a Pictish town here, which was destroyed
in a Viking raid.

'A fort built to curb the Highlander' (Defoe)

From 1650 to 1745 the Highlands were re-fortified, but this time not
by individual clan chiefs but by the government. Inverlochy, at the
south-western end of the Great Glen, was the site of one of these
forts. Begun in 1654 by General Monk, the fort, known as the
'Garrison of Inverlochy', stood on the promontory at the confluence
of the River Nevis with the junction of Loch Eil and Loch Linnhe,
with a bog on its south side and a ditch to the west. The position
was defensive, and could be easily provisioned by sea. The rampart
was probably built of turf, topped by a structure of clay and wattle,
enclosing an irregular pentagon. At the south-east corner was one
full three-pointed artillery bastion, with demi-bastions at the other
four corners (Fig. 42). The fort probably held about 250 troops.

In 1690 General Hugh Mackay of Scourie rebuilt the fort in stone, and named it Fort William in honour of the new king (7.1). Three naval ships and five hired merchant ships brought in men and tools, and, with the sailors as well as the soldiers helping, the fort was constructed in eleven days. It was 'an irregular work of a triangular form, with ditches, glacis and ravelin'. The fort had a bomb-proof magazine, and two bastions mounting fifteen guns, taken off naval ships which arrived with supplies, as there was concern about a possible French attack. HMS *Dartmouth*, a fifth-rate naval ship which was wrecked in 1690 in the Sound of Mull soon after leaving Fort William, provided six of the guns. The officers' quarters were of stone, but the barracks of wood. It was from here that troops were sent to Glencoe in February 1692.

The fort was besieged during the 1715 Jacobite rising, and in 1725 General Wade carried out some repair work on it. In 1745 Fort George at Inverness and Fort Augustus in the Great Glen had fallen to the Jacobites very quickly, and the government was determined that Fort William should not fall as well. In 1746 it was besieged for six weeks by Jacobite forces retreating from Derby, causing considerable damage, until they abandoned the siege and moved on to Culloden. The fort was reconstructed immediately after this, including the building of new barrack blocks (Fig. 10). In 1752 James of the Glen was held here after he was arrested for the Appin Murder.

In the late eighteenth century the fort was damaged when the River Nevis flooded, and this time it was not repaired. In 1792 it was described as 'a small triangular fort . . . well situated for defending the passage by sea'. In the *Old Statistical Account* it is described as 'by no means a place of strength. For these two years past, all the men in it have been only a company of invalids. Besides, some years ago, about a fourth part of the wall was undermined, and swept away by the river Nevis: It has ever since being fast going to ruin'.

A small garrison remained, however, mainly to deter smuggling, until the outbreak of the Crimean War in 1854. After that it was manned by volunteer regiments, on anti-smuggling duties, until 1864,

Fig. 10. View of the fort at Fort William (after an eigtheenth century water-colour)

after which the buildings were sold and used as housing. In 1889 the site was bought by the West Highland Railway for a goods yard, and part of the fort demolished. The officers' accommodation was occupied by railway employees until 1935, and not finally demolished until 1948. All that survives today is the north and west ramparts, and the north-west demi-bastion. A round-arched gateway, dating from the 1690 rebuilding, was re-erected in 1896 at the entrance to The Craigs Burial Ground, at the spot where the first Cameron Highlanders, raised in 1793, were sworn in (Plate 8). Panelling from a room in the Governor's House of the fort was given to the West Highland Museum by the railway company in 1935, and reassembled in a room in the museum two years later. In the early 1970s the River Nevis was diverted, and the remains of the fort are now cut off from the town by the main road. The former parade ground, however, survives as a public open space between the High Street and the Station.

The Town

Keppoch, at the junction of the Glen Roy and Glen Spean, was created a burgh of barony in 1690 under MacIntosh of Torcastle, but it did not develop. Fort William, therefore, is the only burgh in Lochaber. There is a strong local tradition that the town is older than documentary evidence suggests. One story has a burgh which exported skins and fish to Spain, and imported coal and food, but which was in decline by the time the first fort was built. A settlement in the Inverlochy area had been created a burgh of barony in 1618 by George Gordon, marquess of Huntly, and called Gordonsburgh, but this tells us nothing about what was already existing on the site. In 1690, when the fort was renamed Fort William after the new King William of Orange, the adjacent settlement was renamed Maryburgh in honour of his wife, Queen Mary. This town was largely destroyed in the 1745–6 rebellion, and rebuilt soon afterwards, as a single street along the line of the military road.

In the 1730s, on the advice of General Wade, Maryburgh was made the centre for quarter-sessions, and by 1736 a Masonic Lodge had been established. Bishop Pococke, who visited it in 1760, described it as 'a very poor town'. But during the second half of the eighteenth century, in more peaceful times, the town began to grow and flourish, particularly as a port. In the 1778 edition of Defoe's *Tour* the town was described as 'originally intended as a sutlery to the garrisons, and afterwards erected into a barony, in favour of the governor of the fort. The houses are all, by special appointment, built of timber and turf, that they may be easily and suddenly burnt up by the commandant when in danger of becoming a lodgement for an enemy.' It also noted that 'Fort William is surrounded by vast mountains, which occasion almost perpetual rain.'

According to the *Old Statistical Account* in the 1790s, the town had twenty-six masons, twenty-four weavers, eighteen shoemakers, twelve tailors, eleven carpenters, nine shopkeepers, and nine makers of women's clothes. There were also four lawyers, three butchers, three bakers, three surgeons, three wheelwrights, three boatwrights, two coopers, two schoolmasters, two excise men, two innkeepers and one shipwright. There were only two merchants, the same number as there were fiddlers. The town's disadvantages included the lack of a regular weekly market 'for butcher meat and other articles'. The minister suggested that the town needed a tannery, a sawmill (there were six men sawing wood by hand) and a manufactory of coarse woollen cloth. This was because the town was exporting raw wool and then importing the finished cloth: 'thus the English manufacturer and merchant are enriched by the produce of our country, while hundreds of our own people are idle and unemployed throughout the whole year'. A lot of timber was imported, but without a proper quay visiting vessels had to cross to Camusnagaul for shelter in a storm. A quay would only have cost £440, but the merchants could not afford this. One puzzling complaint was the lack of a good supply of fresh water for both the town and the garrison. Despite these problems, however, Fort William was described as 'in a thriving way', and with the patronage of the Gordon family 'is likely to become a distinguished place'. It was in around 1790 that the sheriff court was established.

Another observer in 1792 described it as 'a very handsome village, which has increased rapidly of later years, owing to the spirit and success of the inhabitants, in prosecuting the herring fishery'. John Leyden in 1800 described it as 'a beautiful village by the side of a lake, which, after wandering so long in the wildest parts of the Highlands, we are very much disposed to call a town'. He regarded it as 'much superior to Oban in regularity and beauty' and estimated it had about 1,600 inhabitants. In the 1790s the proprietor, the duke of Gordon, tried unsuccessfully to change its name back to Gordonsburgh.

Different travellers saw the town differently, perhaps influenced by the weather, and the discomfort of the journey endured to reach Fort William. James Hogg in 1803 described it as 'destitute of trade and manufactures, nor was there a vessel in the harbour'. *The Steam Boat Companion and Stranger's Guide to the Western Islands and Highlands of Scotland*, published in 1820, described Fort William as 'but a small place, of consequence only from its custom-house and garrison'. Macculloch in 1824 mentioned the coasting trade, and sheep and cattle fairs, noting that the loss of the garrison had caused economic recession, but the opening of the Caledonian Canal in 1822 was helping the town to revive. Bowman, in 1826, described it as 'a small and poor town . . . the houses are mostly small and mean; and the place has a dull, deserted appearance, though it is a sort of metropolis for the surrounding district'. He commented that there were no gigs for hire, only carts, presumably because of the poor quality of the roads.

A trades directory of 1825, however, described the town as consisting of 'one pretty regular street, embellished with some handsome buildings, the principal of which is the Caledonian Hotel'. It was governed by a baron bailie appointed by the duke of Gordon, the feu superior. A weekly market was held and two annual fairs, and the population was about 700. There were three churches, Church of Scotland, Episcopal and Roman Catholic, a library (established in 1819) and a customs house. However, there were no 'gentry' listed, though there were twenty-six listed for Tobermory, on Mull. The town was a commercial centre for the area, but not yet a social centre.

In 1834 the new feu superior, Sir Duncan Cameron of Fassifern, tried to change the name of the town to Duncansburgh, but it did not catch on, except for the parish church, which still retains the name today. Sir Duncan was responsible for many improvements, including laying out the High Street, with lanes running down to the waterfront. The population in 1835 was about 1,200. 'Tartan among men, and cotton cloth among women, are the common costume.' There was one bank, twenty merchants, three doctors, four lawyers and the sheriff-substitute. But although a market had been established, it was very small. There were two libraries – one religious and one literary, but 'the numerous spirit-shops . . . prove a great snare to those who ought to employ their time in reading'. By 1842 there was a distillery, run by 'Long John' MacDonald (9.14). By 1850 there were two banks, and the town was described as principally inhabited by those engaged in the herring fishery'.

In 1873 Queen Victoria visited the town, and described it as 'small, and, excepting where the good shops are, very dirty, with a very poor population, but all very friendly and enthusiastic'. Two years later it became a police burgh, and in 1892 the Police Commissioners were replaced by a Burgh Council. The *Ordnance Gazetteer* of 1894 described it thus: 'it chiefly consists of three parallel lines of buildings, forming two streets, and containing several good hotels and shops, whilst in the suburbs are a number of handsome villas'. The stone quay had finally been built in 1834, and by the 1890s the town had three banks, a gas works, five fairs and the sheriff court. During the first half of the nineteenth century the town developed a new role as a point of departure for emigrants.

By 1875 the population had risen to about 1,500. Until 1860 the post came from Bonawe – 'one man could carry on his back all the correspondence for Ballachulish, Glencoe, Morvern, Ardnamurchan, and Fort William'. In 1865 Fort William became a postal district, with the mail arriving via Perth and Kingussie (the nearest railway station). The telegraph arrived in 1871. In 1881 the post came by rail to Oban, then on by steamer to Fort William. With the coming of the West Highland Railway in 1894 post could reach Fort William direct by rail, and a new post office was built in 1897. The town had first been lit by oil lamps. In the 1840s these were replaced by gas lamps, until in 1896 Fort William became the first town in Britain to be lit by hydroelectric power.

After the coming of the railway Fort William quickly developed as a tourist centre, and experienced a building boom. In 1920 M.E.M. Donaldson described it as a place 'to which you only go so that you may get away from it and on to somewhere else with all possible speed . . . an ugly little town, compacted of hideous buildings, [which] incongruously defaces the landscape'. But its population had risen to nearly 2,000.

In the 1950s an attempt was made to change the town's name again, incorporating the suburbs of Inverlochy, Banavie, Corpach and Coal, and calling the whole conglomeration Nevisburgh or Abernevis. By 1951 the population had risen to 2,674. In the 1960s Fort William was described as 'a town which has made splendid progress from a garrison centre in the seventeenth century to a modern industrial, commercial and tourist centre'. In 1965 the new Belford Hospital was opened, and in 1973–4 the shore road was built, diverting through traffic from the High Street, which is now pedestrianised. The former parade ground is now a public park. Further north is Jubilee Park, given to the town to celebrate Queen Victoria's Golden Jubilee, but later renamed George V Park. A swimming pool has been built on part of it. Fort William today is a busy town, and a centre from which tourists can explore the West Highlands.

6. ECONOMIC CHANGE AND THE RURAL ECONOMY

By the seventeenth century, although the clan system still prevailed, most day-to-day responsibility for land management had been delegated from the landowners to their tacksmen (main tenants). The mainstay of the economy was subsistence agriculture, with grazing increasing in importance, as cattle were the main exportable product. This made the change to sheep during the late eighteenth and early nineteenth centuries relatively simple. There was some small-scale iron and charcoal making, and some timber was exported for fuel and charcoal. There was some fishing, but the best sea-fishing was still dominated by the Dutch.

Agriculture

> The climate of the north-west coast of Scotland generally unfits it for the purposes of agriculture. (*New Statistical Account*, Glenelg, 1836)

Clearly the better areas of land had been farmed whenever people inhabited this area throughout history, but evidence for farming before the eighteenth century is fragmentary. The *Old Statistical Account* provides snapshots of a period of transition, with some lands held as jointly tenanted farmsteads, while others had made the change to larger individual farms. An increasing number of rural inhabitants were to become wage-earners rather than small tenant farmers or smallholders. The creation of sheep-walks led to a more intensive use of the remaining land, and also provided an impetus for emigration.

According to the *Old Statistical Account* for Kilmallie, before 1764 'all the arable land was carefully cultivated, and sowed, mostly with oats'. Cattle, and a few sheep and goats, were grazed on common grazing, and the tenant farmers 'had plenty of milk, butter and cheese', and 'lived very comfortably'. In return, they were always ready to perform for their landlords every kind of service. As the population grew dramatically in the later eighteenth century, poor and marginal land had to be exploited, but even if tenants could afford equipment and animals, some land was too rough to be worked in any other way than by hand. Any material which could be used as manure was valuable. Edward Burt in 1726 described how, not far from Fort William, he had seen 'women with a little horse-dung brought upon their backs, in creels, or baskets, from that garrison; and on their knees, spreading it with their hands upon the land, and even breaking the balls, that every part of the little spot might have its due proportion'. The same women cut hay by knife from the roadside verges.

Crops grown at the end of the eighteenth century included oats, bear (barley) and potatoes, which once they caught on were (until the potato blight of the 1840s) regarded as a crop less susceptible to the vagaries of the weather than grain. John Knox in 1786 reported that grain was easily spoiled by the wet weather, 'roots, vegetables, sallads, common fruits, being less hurt by the rains, can be raised in any quantities', and 'potatoes serve, throughout the Highlands, as a substitute for grain'. In the *Old Statistical Account* many parishes reported that agriculture was severely hampered by the wind and rain. In Glenelg, for example, hay should have been harvested in July or August and grain crops in September or October, but sometimes 'owing to the deluges of rain that too often fall about this season of the year, the hay as well as other crops are often not secured till November'. In Morvern, white oats had been introduced, and produced a better yield, but were at greater risk from rains in July and August and autumnal storms. In Kilmonivaig 'the wetness of the climate is an invincible bar to the raising of corn'. Because of this many, including 'gentlemen tacksmen, have now turned their attention to grazing and rearing of cattle'. The countryside was best adapted to grazing, and arable farming was attempted through necessity not choice. Even in good years the supply of grain did not last until the next crop was harvested, and oatmeal had to be bought in.

Arable land was cultivated in strips, called rigs, with furrows between them for drainage. This enabled the best land to be shared out fairly among communal farmers, as well as helping with drainage. The remains of 'rig and furrow' can still be seen at many places in the Highland landscape. Potatoes gave a higher yield per acre than grain crops, which was another factor which helped sustain for a while the rapidly increasing population of the Highlands. The very poorest land could be used for growing potatoes by creating 'lazy-beds', building up beds using any available manure, but particularly seaweed. These can also still be spotted, usually much smaller and more isolated than areas of rig and furrow. The minister of Morvern claimed that potatoes grown in lazy-beds could produce a tenfold return.

According to Thomas Pennant in 1769, 'The great produce of Lochaber is cattle'. The main cash crop for the tenant farmer was black cattle, a hardy breed which could live outside all year round. When three years old they were sold to drovers, who walked them to markets in Crieff or Falkirk. The minister of Glenelg reported that they fetched two to three guineas (£2.10–£3.15) each. In many areas 'the cattle ranged through the hills as high up as the grass grew, and it was necessary, during summer, to follow them . . . to milk them there, and make up stores of butter and cheese for winter use' (Norman Macleod). This was mainly done by women and children, living in temporary stone or wooden huts known as 'shielings'.

Any profit on the sale of cattle would be spent on things the farmer could not grow or make for himself, such as shoes, and items such as ironware for house and farm. Not all rural communities could sustain full-time craftsmen, such as blacksmiths or leather-workers, so many had to become multi-skilled. Other purchases included salt, and timber for building. Morvern, for example, exported cattle, horses, sheep, wool, kelp, timber and bark (for tanning), and imported meal, tanned leather, iron, tar, ropes, smearing butter (the predecessor of sheep dip), and miscellaneous merchant goods.

Sheep had always been kept in small numbers for their wool, used for making the family's clothes. By the late eighteenth century some farms had been totally taken over for sheep, which produced a good profit with minimum labour and tools, which suited landowners struggling to make a profit from large but unproductive estates. As the minister of Kilmallie explained, 'they require a smaller number of hands to tend them, than black cattle; can graze in places where these would not venture, and yield a greater produce. This, it will be acknowledged, is a strong temptation to proprietors, who value *money* more than *men*, to encourage *sheep-farming*.' Glengarry's tenants, for example, shipped their wool to Greenock, Dumbarton and Liverpool. 10,000 to 15,000 stones (63.5–95.25 tonnes) of wool was being exported from Fort William, mainly to Liverpool. By the time of the *Old Statistical Account* sheep already dominated the Lochaber area, and the population was beginning to decline. An agricultural report published in 1812 recorded that agriculture was generally backward, except in Ardgour, and particularly Strontian, where an agricultural society had been formed.

Small hardy horses were kept for transport and for pulling simple ploughs. A few goats were kept, and some cattle, both mainly for their milk. In Kilmallie parish in the 1790s there were 6,000 black cattle, 500 horses, 1,000 goats and 60,000 sheep (first introduced in 1764). In Kilmonivaig there were 60,000 sheep, 1,500 black cattle and 500 horses. In Ardnamurchan 300 farmers had 20 carts and 42 ploughs, 400 draught horses, 7,546 cattle, 45,350 sheep, 2,300 goats and 50 'swine'. The basic diet consisted of oatmeal, potatoes, fish, and dairy products if available. Grain and potatoes were grown to feed the family.

The population of Ardnamurchan in the 1790s was 4,542. As well as the 300 farmers, there were 90 weavers, 76 miners (and mine labourers), 35 tailors, 19 house and boat carpenters, 9 shopkeepers, 9 'whisky-house keepers', 9 masons, 7 smiths, 6 millers, 5 shoemakers,

3 schoolmasters (and 4 private teachers), and 2 merchants. There were no doctors or lawyers. The transport of goods into and out of the area was difficult and slow, though there was a small elite who created a demand for imported consumer goods. Much came by sea, but even water transport added greatly to its original cost. There were few roads suitable for wheeled transport before the mid nineteenth century, but much was carried on foot or on pack pony, and distribution could be achieved in several short stages by local carriers. Creels on the back, or panniers on a pony, or simple sleds, could be used to move goods over rough terrain. Wherever possible local resources had to be used. Shell-sand was used as a fertiliser, for example, where lime was not available. The nearest markets to Lochaber were Inverness, Tobermory (on Mull) and Oban.

Rare patches of relatively flat ground near settlements, now often public open spaces, were often once the sites of cattle fairs. Examples include the present playing field at Lochaline (NM 676 452). Fairs seem to have developed in the early nineteenth century, as they are not mentioned in the *Old Statistical Account*, but are usually listed in the *Second Statistical Account*. An almanac of 1802 lists fairs at Ardnamurchan (19 May and 15 October), Sunart (22 May and 18 October) and Gordonsburgh (second Wednesdays in June and November). Those around 1840 include two at Fort William (June and November), two at Duror (April and October), two at Strontian (May and October), and two at Arisaig and in Morvern.

Mills seem to have come late to this area. There may well have been simple horizontal mills for which little evidence now survives. But many settlements were too remote from estate mills to be forced to use them, and corn was ground by hand, as had been done since prehistoric times. Thomas Pennant in 1769 saw at Kinlochleven 'a sort of portable mill, made of two stones about two feet broad, thin at the edges, and a little thicker in the middle. In the centre of the upper stone is a hole to pour in the corn, and a peg by way of handle. The whole is placed on a cloth; the grinder pours the corn into the hole with one hand, and with the other turns round the upper stone with a very rapid motion, while the meal runs out at the sides on the cloth.' The minister of Lismore and Appin in 1841 noted that hand querns were still in use in Kingairloch.

Steam transport offered more opportunity for exports. In the 1830s, for example, great quantities of eggs were sent from Ardnamurchan to Glasgow. During the nineteenth century agriculture continued to change. Wool ceased to be a profitable crop once Australia began to export a superior product. Some estates eventually accepted that agriculture was not profitable, and ran at a loss providing recreation for the rich, particularly deer stalking, shooting and fishing.

Some displaced tenants and cottars were settled in crofting townships, villages laid out with small areas of land attached to each house. By the later nineteenth century improved communications, and increased reading of newspapers and periodicals, allowed the plight of poor crofters in parts of the Highlands to be publicised. The first Crofter's Commission reported in 1884, and provides us with valuable information about actual living conditions and forms of tenancy. The resulting Crofters' Holdings (Scotland) Act of 1886 gave crofters in designated areas security of tenure, and compensation for improvements if they gave up their tenancy. Subsequent legislation has increased the protection afforded to small tenants in the Highlands. Crofting still survives in some places, generally either through amalgamation of holdings to create small farms, or through combining crofting with another paid occupation. But in general farms are large, but struggling because of the quality of the land. There have been various experiments, including the great Glen Cattle Ranch, created by Joseph Hobbs, an Englishman who had originally made his money in Canada. In the 1940s he sold his distillery business and set up the cattle ranch, improving the land considerably. Some of the labelled ranch buildings can be seen from the road between Fort William and Spean Bridge.

Early photographs show a landscape much barer than it is today. More of the grazing cattle and sheep are now kept within clearly defined fields, and they are fewer in number. The lack of arable farming, and the reduction in numbers of grazing animals, has led to the spread of bracken, and it takes well-balanced grazing, and cutting grass for hay or silage, to keep fields free from bracken. More native woodland is now being allowed to regenerate, by excluding grazing animals. The maintenance of the Highland landscape in the form in which we are used to perceiving it is an increasing problem, and needs agricultural activities to continue to both use and maintain it. But without subsidies hill-farming is not economically viable.

Emigration and Clearances

During the later eighteenth century some clan chiefs adopted a typical lifestyle of the land-owning classes, and were more outward-looking. Cameron of Locheil, for example, held land in North America and the Caribbean. The colonies attracted others, particularly the tenant farmer class. The first emigrant ship left Maryburgh (Fort William) in 1773. Most landowners deplored the loss of people from their estates, and were therefore stimulated to improve the employment they could offer locally. The government also played its part. Although its road-building programme was started for military purposes, it did serve to open up the country to new ideas and new economic developments and opportunities. One writer in 1792 claimed that road building 'had removed the prejudices which formerly narrowed their minds, and fascinated them to clannish predilections and subordination'. But it meant people were not so happy to live in remote places at subsistence level. 'The natives now feel wants and inconveniences which formerly gave them no uneasiness'; being aware of what the wider world had to offer led to discontent and raised expectations.

Emigration therefore pre-dated the clearing of land for sheep farming. Once it had started, people left not just because of problems at home, such as increased rents, but because of 'the flattering accounts received from their friends in America'. Not all emigrants went as far. Some simply moved into Fort William, or went south to Greenock and Glasgow. Large numbers of men left because they enlisted in the army. In 1756, 750 men from the parish of Kilmallie had enlisted, mostly in Highland regiments, which quickly became an important asset to the British army. Those who came home brought back new ideas. More and more people wanted to be able to afford consumer goods, and were less willing to live on potatoes in damp turf huts. In 1843 the minister of Morvern could write: 'There are as yet no roads, no adequate means of religious or moral instruction, no resident medical practitioner, no regular or steady employment for the people'. He therefore reluctantly endorsed emigration because he could see no viable alternative.

During the eighteenth and nineteenth centuries estate owners were looking for ways to improve the profitability of their estates, and the most obvious was sheep farming. Many did try to provide land or employment for those forcibly removed. In Glenelg, for example, the minister suggested that it might be profitable to establish a woollen cloth factory, or a net manufactory. In 1828 Sir James Milles Riddell, of Ardnamurchan, was awarded a gold medal by the Highland Society 'for his benevolent and patriotic exertions in promoting the establishment of the manufactory of straw-plait upon his estate at Strontian'. But, just as in the Lowlands, most such schemes never got off the ground, or only lasted a few years. Most landowners eventually resorted to clearing their land of the cottars who paid no rent.

Serious clearance of the land began in the early nineteenth century, as sheep farming took off, and small tenants were evicted from some upland areas to make way for imported sheep ('big sheep', in contrast to the smaller indigenous ones) and imported Lowland shepherds. According to William Larkin in 1818, 'the sheep farming system in Glencoe has done the work of extirpation of the inhabitants more effectively than the Massacre of 1692'.

> In vain I tried the Highlanders to keep
> from being devour'd by flocks of Lowland sheep;
> But rage for rent extinguished every thought
> For men who bravely had our battles fought.
>
> (George Dempster, 1809)

There were several waves. At first people were moved from inland glens to the coast, where subsistence was theoretically easier. But without the kelp industry, which collapsed after 1820, even the coast could not sustain everyone, and clearances continued. The potato famine of the 1840s was the final straw. People had to be induced to leave the land. Some were rehoused on the worst bits of land on the estate, while others were offered financial help to emigrate to North America and by the 1850s Australia as well. After the potato famine the settlements of Doirlinn, Scardoish, Portabhata, Briaig and Mingarry in Ardnamurchan, for example, were among those emptied by emigration to Australia. The inhabitants of Caolas, in Moidart, are said to have emigrated in 1852 to Australia, mainly because of persuasion by their priest.

The land-owning class was also changing fast. Some went bankrupt, while the luckier ones married heiresses and moved out of the Highlands. The native landowners who remained spent more and more time away, living the life of a gentleman. And more and more estates were being bought, inherited or acquired through marriage by Englishmen, often as one component of a wider landholding. A writer in 1840 described Lord Cranstoun as regarding his Highland estate 'as simply entitling him to a wider round of pleasure; and in the fashionable saloons of London this English nobleman has squandered in a few hours of luxury . . . the hundreds which cost the poor people of Arisaig a year of toil and privation to collect'.

Landowners had different views of clearance. While many regarded it as a good thing, or as the only solution to their problems, at least a few wondered whether it was inevitable. Lord Howard of Glossop, who owned Doirlinn, on Loch Shiel, between 1871 and 1883, said that 'the real way to improve the condition of the people was . . . to enlarge their holdings, and to give them facilities for maintaining an increase of stock. A steady pursuance of this system would, he believed, ultimately tend to convert crofters into a well-to-do class of small farmers . . . Although not averse to their emigrating to the colonies, he had a positive horror of Highland families being drafted into the cities where, as he alleged, they had little chance of escaping contamination both in their health and in their morals'.

Academic studies have demonstrated, however, that the folk memory of the clearances is not always fair. There is a tendency for more blame to be put on absentee landowners than on those who still lived locally, particularly those of long standing. The reality is a much more even picture. Even at subsistence level, the land could not support so many people after the collapse of the kelp industry. Agricultural workers were being dispossessed all over Britain, though perhaps not so brutally. If sheep had not been brought in, people would still have had to leave the land, just more gradually. And more and more people wanted to live at a better level, and enjoy the benefits of the growing consumer society. Once transport improved and more people saw what life was like in the rest of Scotland and beyond, change was inevitable.

Fishing

From historical records it seems that there have always been plenty of fish off the coasts of the west Highlands, and in the seventeenth and eighteenth centuries many foreign boats came to exploit these resources. Travellers, and those sent on behalf of the government or organisations such as the Highland Society, all commented on the lack of offshore fishing by locals, and particularly the lack of exploitation of the summer herring shoals. This was variously put down to lack of capital for boats and nets, lack of salt with which to process the fish, lack of convenient markets, or lack of initiative. The British Fisheries Society sent out people to investigate sites on which new fishing villages could be founded. None of these was in Lochaber, although they established one at Tobermory, on Mull. None of these villages fulfilled their original purpose. People were unwilling to put all their eggs in one basket, and preferred to have a smallholding as well as working as fishermen. Most of the settlements survived, but with a broader-based economy, and developed much more slowly than originally envisaged.

The problem with herring fishing was that it needed expensive nets, and salt and barrels to preserve the surplus. Salt was a taxable commodity, held in bonded stores, and the government would only set one up in a remote area if there was enough demand. As the herring season was only a few weeks a year, the whole business was not viable. So the fish were exploited by boats from other areas such as the Clyde. Some herring were caught, however, either for domestic consumption, or sold immediately to larger fishing boats in the area. The herring fishery boomed during the nineteenth century, though Lochaber played little part in it. There was a small commercial herring fishery based in Fort William in the mid nineteenth century. In the late nineteenth century visiting herring boats employed local men during season, and girls followed the herring fleet round the coast. Salmon was also caught and, like herring, salted and packed in barrels for export. But attempts to expand salmon fishing were not very successful. In Morvern, for example, the fishery at the head of Lochaline was successful, but attempts in the 1830s 'to establish salmon fishings along the sea coasts' met with 'little success'. The *New Statistical Account* records salmon caught in stake nets at Kingairloch, and some dredging for oysters. The *Old Statistical Account* records that dogfish (and larger sharks if available) were caught to extract oil from their livers. In the later eighteenth century basking shark fishing started. Only the liver was used. This fishery declined after 1820, though experienced a brief revival in the mid twentieth century.

The nineteenth century also saw a gradual expansion of commercial white fishing, and this continued to grow after the decline of herring fishing from the 1920s. Mallaig, now the second largest settlement in Lochaber, started life as a fishing village, with only three houses in 1901. Then the railway came, took over the only flat bit of land and built the first pier here. Before this the main fishing port in the area had been Tarbet, on Loch Nevis. By the early 1970s Mallaig was the most important herring fishing port in Europe, handling a third of the British catch. Although fishing is now in decline, Mallaig is also a ferry port, serving Skye and the Small Isles.

However, anyone who lived on or near the coast did a little fishing to supplement a meagre and boring diet. Farmers on the west coast, and on loch shores, needed boats anyway, in order to get in supplies and take goods to market. Others shared boats, and went fishing close to shore, in sheltered waters such as sea lochs. Most used handlines. The minister of Glenelg in the 1790s mentioned local catches of skate, ling, and cod, but mainly saithe, which 'in summer is chiefly the support of the poor people'. There were salmon, trout and other fish in the rivers, but these belonged to the landowners, who regarded their rights as commercial property, which they often leased to enterprises from outside the area. The minister of Kilmallie mentioned a short-lived trade in salted salmon, exported from Fort William to Aberdeen and Greenock, from where they were sent on to Ostend and Bilbao. Other fish caught in the Fort William area included cod, lythe, saithe, skate, flounders, mackerel, whiting and a few haddock, also eels and sturgeon. Long-lines were baited with mussels or herring. The minister of Morvern listed salmon, herring, saithe, red cod, skate, lythe, flounder, mackerel, sea perch, dogfish, gurnet, eels, and small salmon and trout.

As well as fishing at sea, there was food to be gathered from the foreshore without the need for boats. The minister of Morvern said that his parishioners caught 'a variety of shell-fish, such as, oysters, cockles, lobsters, crabs, muscles, limpets and periwinkles, spout fish, etc'. 'There are also found marine vegetables, dulse, and slake, which are much esteemed by those who are in the habit of using them.' One way to exploit shallow-water fish and crustaceans was to build fish-traps. These were of two types. There were 'cruives' at river mouths, particularly to catch salmon as they moved inland to spawn. These consisted of wattle fences built out from both banks, with a narrow gap at the centre across which a net or basket could be placed. These were so successful that the owners of river fisheries objected. In the

1790s, for example, it was reported that salmon catches near Fort William had been killed by cruives at river mouths. As a result, all static fishing engines were banned in the 1860s. The other type of fish-trap consisted of wattle or stone walls on the foreshore, with or without a gap, which trapped fish as the tide retreated. Surviving examples in Lochaber tend to be of stone. They look like semicircles on the beach, thought they are often made up of short stretches of straight walls (Plate 20).

Forestry

It is now generally accepted that the deforestation of Scotland began as soon as people lived here. The hunter-gatherers of the Mesolithic probably had relatively little effect on the environment, but once farming began land was cleared to grow crops, and grazing animals stopped trees regenerating. Wood was the main fuel and building material, but for these uses could be harvested sustainably. There is good evidence that from prehistoric times woodland was actively managed. Some was coppiced to produce straight poles used for building creel houses and wattle fences, while some was pollarded, or coppiced at a higher level on the trunk. This produced the same result, while allowing animals to be grazed underneath without damaging the trees.

By the eighteenth century there was still much native woodland remaining in Lochaber, partly because it was not of high enough quality to have been exploited commercially to export for building house and ships. In 1746, however, as part of the punitive measures taken against Jacobite supporters, the woods along the Morvern coast were deliberately burned. There was also commercial felling in Glencoe and Ardgour, with little or no regeneration, as landowners increasingly came to see timber as a short-term cash crop. The minister of Morvern in 1843 reported that the woods used to be coppiced until the Argyll lands were sold in 1819, implying that after that date coppicing was discontinued.

The minister of Kilmallie in the 1790s reported that there were some good trees, but even if they were close to the shore, the roads were so bad that timber was difficult to extract: 'the trees that grow naturally, are oak, fir, birch, ash, mountain-ash, holly, elm, wild green, hazel, and the Scotch poplar. Those planted are larix, spruce, silver fir, beech, plane and fruit trees.' In Morvern the proprietors of the woods around Lochaline and beside Loch Sunart 'benefit themselves much by selling them off to the Lorn furnace company or others for charcoal, etc., the manufacturing of which must be supposed very serviceable to the poor of this and the neighbouring parishes'. Charcoal was produced from coppiced wood, and did not necessarily mean that large areas were felled. It was also labour-intensive, involving cutting, piling, burning, transporting and the peeling of bark. Macdonnell of Glengarry, like many landowners, sold timber for making charcoal for ironworks. Charcoal-burning platforms can be found in woodland all over the area.

The First World War demonstrated Britain's lack of timber, and in 1919 the Foresty Commission was established to ensure that, if war came again, Britain would be self-sufficient in timber for industrial uses such as pit-props. Many estates put up for sale because their owners or heirs had died in the war were bought by the Forestry Commission and planted with fast-growing conifers. The Commission is still today a major landowner and major employer in the Highlands, although it does now plant a wider variety of trees, and allows its plantations to be used for recreational purposes. There is also a recent development of locally managed 'community woodlands', and more estates are replanting broadleaf trees.

Castles, Country Houses and their Owners

The Comyns built castles to defend their lands, including Inverlochy, while the Lords of the Isles built a chain of castles in the thirteenth century, including Ardtornish (4.1) (Figs 4 and 26), Mingary (4.10) (Fig. 28) and Tioram (4.11) (Plate 10; Fig. 29). The last two are true

Fig. 11. Kinlochaline Castle from the south-west (from MacGibbon & Ross, Castellated and Domestic Architecture)

castles, while Ardtornish, the seat of power, was a hall-house, though well defended by its position on a promontory. Some if not most of these medieval castle sites had probably been defended locations intermittently since prehistoric times. The fourteenth century saw improvements to some castles, including Tioram. More settled times in the fourteenth and fifteenth centuries saw the building of tower houses, which although defensible are really family homes. Examples of this type include Glensanda (4.5) and Kinlochaline (4.8) (Fig. 11).

Shipborne artillery sent by government forces rendered all these castles redundant as places of defence, and some saw a final use as government garrisons. Without a defensive purpose, the castles were both too expensive to maintain, and too uncomfortable to live in. Some were gradually converted to houses, but remained the centre of the estate, or, in the case of Inverlochy, the seat of the sheriff. In most cases, however, a new house was built, often in a less exposed location, and with space around it for gardens and trees for shelter and privacy. But more so than in other parts of Scotland, the move from castle to house was often disrupted or delayed by political, religious or dynastic instability, as well as by lack of money.

There is fragmentary evidence, however, that in the disturbed times of the sixteenth and seventeenth centuries some castles were succeeded by much smaller buildings, sometimes of wood, on islands or protected by moats or palisades. Lachlan Mhor Mackintosh is said to have constructed a crannog on Loch Lochy in 1580, as a base for controlling Lochaber. At Tigh Dige, Annaheilt, near Strontian (NM 817 627), the MacIans are said to have had a hall-house within a stockade, surrounded by a ditch. The house built in the early sixteenth century by the MacDonalds of Keppoch stood on a mound (probably natural), surrounded by a moat. (NN 270 807). The Camerons of Locheil are said to have lived on Eilean nan Craobh, in Loch Eil (NN 089 763) during the sixteenth and seventeenth centuries, in a timber house, of which no trace now survives. And there is evidence for seventeenth century reuse of some prehistoric crannogs, such as Eilean Tigh Na Slige, Loch Treig (NN 347 768). In the sixteenth century the Keppoch chiefs are said to have held council meetings and feasts there.

Even when times became more settled, Highland estates did not in general yield enough profit, particularly in cash rather than kind, for their owners to indulge in major building projects. Lochaber has very few country houses dating from the seventeenth century, because the area was unsettled, and some lairds were absentees. Even in the eighteenth century, some lairds' houses were surprisingly small and of vernacular build. John Leyden in 1800 reported that 'MacDonall of Glengarry has constructed, on the side of Loch Nevis . . . a wicker house in the ancient manner, to serve as a hunting-box'. The minister of Glenelg in 1836 described the two main rooms as being wattle-walled, with no ceilings, and 'the floor is of clay and hard sand'. It was cruck-framed, the couples 'rising from the ground and meeting in massive arches overhead'. According to Joseph Mitchell: 'The only houses superior to those of the peasantry were a few two-storeyed dwellings and improved huts, lined with dressed pine planks, and sometimes furnished with beds shut up at one side of the room, as is common in France. Several of these rooms so lined, with stone hearths and good peat fire-places, formed a very comfortable abode.'

The houses which were built by 1746, often small and simple, were then destroyed as part of the widespread reprisals after Culloden. These included Glen Nevis House, the headquarters of Cameron of Locheil and MacDonald of Keppoch during the rising. Rebuilding began slowly, while the very few houses which survived the destruction of 1746 were given classical detailing in the later eighteenth century. Most rebuilding in the late eighteenth and early nineteenth centuries was on a fairly modest scale. By the end of the eighteenth century the main landowner in the parish of Glenelg was the Macdonnell of Glengarry; in Kilmallie, the Camerons (of Locheil, Glen Nevis, Fassifern and Loch Leven); in Ardgour there were still Macleans, while the duke of Gordon, the feu superior of Fort William, was non-resident, as were many other proprietors, including the four main landowners in Morvern.

Some tried to continue to live in the style of the older clan chiefs, but usually with disastrous results. The fifteenth and last resident chief of the Macdonnells of Glengarry, Alastair Ranaldson Macdonnell, was a friend of Sir Walter Scott, and his portrait, by Raeburn, hangs in the National Gallery in Edinburgh. 'He kept open house and ignored bank-books, raised and commanded the Glengarry Fencibles, had a fiery temper, welcomed George IV to Edinburgh with a lordly gesture, quarrelled with a gentleman at a ball in Inverness, fought a duel thereafter on the links at Fort George, killed his rival, was tried for murder and acquitted, being indebted for this good luck to the eloquence of his counsel, the famous Harry Erskine' (Ratcliffe Barnett). He died in 1828 when leaping ashore from the shipwrecked steamer *Stirling Castle* at Inverscaddle near Ardgour. His estates had to be sold to pay his debts, and his son emigrated.

Whereas some other parts of Argyll saw a building boom in the 1830s and 1840s, in this area major rebuilding generally did not start until the second half of the nineteenth century. In 1842 the minister of Kilmonivaig stated that Invergarry House was the only mansion in the parish. A few of the old families survived, usually where the land was most fertile, as for example Cameron of Locheil and the MacDonalds of Keppoch. The nineteenth century saw great changes in the Highlands. The early part of the century saw the sale of many estates in Lochaber, as many traditional landowning families had left or gone bankrupt. At this stage some estates became subdivided. Some of their lands were bought by absentee landlords who put in flocks of sheep and English overseers. When sheep ceased to be so profitable, the lands changed hands yet again.

While a few mansions, such as Achnacarry (6.1) (Fig. 39), were the rebuilt seats of the old clan chiefs, the majority were symbols of the new money which moved into the Highlands during the nineteenth century and into the early twentieth, with *nouveau riche* southerners buying estates first for farming, but increasingly for recreation and sport. Rich industrialists looking for holiday homes were not looking to make large profits from their estates, indeed some tolerated continued losses, provided they and their friends could be entertained and given pleasure by the landscape itself, and the sports of shooting and fishing. Estates were merged, and as a result an increasing number of houses were built on new sites. The vast lands of Ardnamurchan, for example, had no big house, with the eighteenth-century owners, if resident, living in Strontian. It was 1898 before a relatively central house was built on the estate, at Glenborrodale. The sheer size of some of these late Victorian houses is best symbolised by Glencoe House (6.13) which now, despite the loss of two wings, is large enough to be used as a hospital. The style of many of these new houses is 'baronial', good examples being Glengarry Castle (1866) (6.14), Kinlochmoidart House (1885) (6.19) and Glenborrodale Castle (1898) (6.12). And the logic of siting changed. Ardtornish Castle, for example, on its exposed headland, was replaced by an eighteenth century laird's house, set further back and sheltered by deliberately planted trees, while the castle ruins became part of its designed landscape, approached along a tree-lined avenue. Eventually, with the merger of estates, this house was replaced by a larger one three miles away at the head of Loch Aline (6.3) (Fig. 40)). This location was more central, more sheltered and more accessible to the new road network, and with plenty of space for outbuildings and gardens, including a river for water power.

Another feature of the later nineteenth century was the shooting lodge. These were new buildings, often well into the hills, away from the heart of an estate. At first they were fairly simply furnished, being intended solely for the temporary accommodation of sporting parties. Joseph Mitchell described Glenquoich Lodge as 'furnished in the simplest manner, with cane-bottomed chairs, and iron bedsteads. The bedrooms were small but numerous, and the whole system of living was simple and rational . . . the gentlemen were early on the mountain side, while the ladies occupied themselves in boating, driving, walking, writing, sketching, and quiet gossip'. Some lodges, however, were soon embellished and designed to impress.

With the 'big house', particularly by the nineteenth century, came a range of domestic offices, agricultural buildings, and ancillary buildings such as stables and coach-houses. Some estates also built sets of matching estate cottages, as for example the concrete buildings designed by Samuel Barham for Ardtornish estate (Plate 26), or the lodges on estates such as Kinlochmoidart. Some estates also built roads and bridges, and piers, ferry houses and such improvements to the maritime infrastructure as would help themselves and their guests. For many of the new large houses were on or near the coast, and used maritime transport for building materials and furnishings, and then for bringing in food, coal and other necessaries. There are records of several tons of furniture being ordered from Glasgow for Ardtornish House, and being delivered by sea.

The First World War saw the death of many young men of all classes. As a result of the loss of sons, many estates came on the market, and were bought by the newly established Forestry Commission. A few large houses have become hospitals or hotels, and a number have been demolished. While land in the Highlands has retained its value, the largest houses have become uneconomic anachronisms.

Rural settlement and housing

The traditional form of settlement in this area was a randomly sited group of houses and byres, with no streets or gardens. Cottages were often built with the door facing east, or facing other buildings, and with as much shelter as possible from the prevailing wind. They generally consisted of one room with a central hearth, with low walls of wicker faced with turf, or later of stone. The walls had rounded corners, and a low thatched roof was supported by timber crucks. The roof timbers were the only parts which had any value, and were reused when a house was rebuilt or a family relocated. Thatch was of whatever material was most readily available, such as heather, turf, or reeds. There was no ceiling inside, so the thatch absorbed the smoke from the fire, and every year was stripped off and used as fertiliser for the fields. Thomas Pennant in 1769 wrote 'The houses of the peasants in Lochaber are the most wretched that can be imagined; framed of upright poles, which are wattled; the roof is formed of boughs like a wigwam, and the whole is covered with sods; so that in this moist climate their cottages have a perpetual and much finer verdure than the rest of the country'.

In *Reminiscences of a Highland Parish*, Norman Macleod wrote of early nineteenth century Morvern, 'these huts were of the most primitive description. They were built of loose stones and clay, the walls were thick, the door low, the rooms numbered one only, or in more aristocratic cases two. The floor was clay; the peat fire was built in the middle of the floor, and the smoke, when amiable and not bullied by a sulky wind, escaped quietly and patiently through a hole in the roof. The window was like a porthole, part of it generally filled with glass and part with peat. One bed, sometimes two, with clean home-made sheets, blankets, and counterpane; a "dresser" with bowls and plate, a large chest, and a corner full of peat, filled up the space beyond the circle about the fire. Upon the rafters above, black as ebony from peat reek, a row of hens and chickens with a stately cock roosted in a paradise of heat'.

During the eighteenth and early nineteenth centuries turf walls were replaced by stone. The next change was the construction of stone gable ends, with built-in fireplaces either in the gables or in a central stone dividing wall. In order to alter existing buildings some cottages had their walls heightened and the round corners corbelled out to become square. But most were totally rebuilt, with the stone walls now mortared and draught-proof for the first time. In 1920 M.E.M. Donaldson described Sanna, at the western extremity of Ardnamurchan, thus:

> Most of the cottages are drystone built, and reed-thatched by the crofters themselves; one, at least, is over a hundred years old, and every one, from the oldest to the newest, has for water supply the nearest burn. All these older cottages are of the 'but and ben' type, but all now have chimneys, consisting of cones of thatch. Though in some cottages the floor is still only of beaten earth, all are scrupulously clean and tidy, like their owners . . . Often in the cottages you see evidences of the skill, ingenuity, and industry of the crofters in their simple furniture – box-bed, table, chairs, cupboard, and dresser – all home-made and often out of driftwood. This is one of the greatest boons to dwellers in this treeless country.

She herself in 1927 built a single-storey house at Sanna of granite, thatched with heather, but much larger than a normal croft house. She built it 'to shew others how the beauty of the old Highland fashion and its fitness in this scenery can consort with every comfort needful in these days'. It burned down in 1947, and the experiment has not been repeated.

Wicker or turf houses leave little or no trace in the landscape. But stone buildings do. Many of the deserted settlements which can be found all over Lochaber date to the first half of the nineteenth century, if not later. They generally consist of tiny stone-walled cottages, often with cruck slots in their walls (though because the walls were thinnest at these points, this is often where they have collapsed

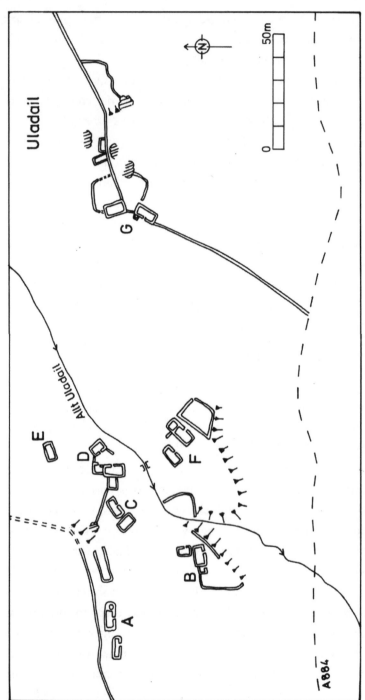

Fig. 12. Plan of the deserted settlement at Uladail, Morvern (Jennie Robertson) (8.24)

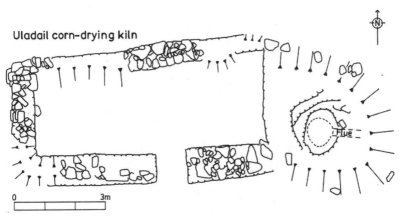

Fig. 13. A barn with attached corn-drying kiln, Uladail, Morvern (Jennie Robertson) (8.24)

to the greatest extent). Associated with them may be byres, corn-drying kilns, small walled kail-yards (vegetable gardens) and simple horizontal mills (Figs 12 and 13). Many examples of 'improved' stone cottages with chimneys can still be seen, both ruined and in use, and a pair in Glencoe village now house a folk museum, established in 1967 (NN 102 589: OS 41).

There were some better houses. In 1800 John Leyden wrote 'Strontian is the principal village of this district, and far exceeded my expectation, as it contains some very elegant houses which I did not hope to see in so wild a scene'. Looking down from the mines, he could see, between the village and the mines, 'above fifty huts . . . surrounded with patches of corn and potato beds, from which the people chiefly derive their sustenance'. In 1834 the houses built for the slate workers at Ballachulish were of stone and lime, with slate roofs, with three rooms, all with plastered walls. But such houses, provided by industrialists to house skilled workers, were the exception.

Another type of settlement site which may be prehistoric, but is little understood, is the recessed platform. It is suggested that these may be foundations for round huts. They are found in many places, and while some are for charcoal burning, others appear to have been domestic or agricultural, and some such may have been reused later

Fig. 14. Large barn or wool store, 1851, Achranich, later Ardtornish (8.2)

for charcoal burning because they were already there. A number have been identified during a recent study of the Sunart oakwoods, for example at Ardery (NM 755 620: OS 40). A few eighteenth-century settlement sites survive, usually in remote places. One example is Airigh Shamhraidh, the predecessor to Kingairloch House, where a house, enclosures and field systems survive (NM 842 494: OS 49).

During the nineteenth century farmhouses were rebuilt, larger and solider, with mortared stone walls and slate roofs, normally facing south (and sometimes retaining the older cottage as a wing at right-angles). By the last decade of the eighteenth century there were twenty-eight houses in Ardnamurchan with slate roofs. Farms also acquired purpose-built steadings. Agricultural buildings were small and simple. There are a few late eighteenth- or early nineteenth-century farm steadings, such as the one near Ardtornish Castle. But most date from the later nineteenth century. The largest and most ornate buildings belong to large estates, as for example the enormous stone barn built at Achranich in 1851 (8.2) (Fig. 14). A large steading is a sign of good arable land.

For fuel, those who could afford it imported coal, otherwise peat and firewood could be gathered. Some areas had good supplies of peat, others were not so fortunate. The minister of Glenelg said their peat was poor because of the high rainfall, and was also some distance from the settlements. In Kilmallie there was plenty of peat, but it was so time-consuming to gather it that if duty were removed from coal it would be worth buying it instead. In Morvern, too, 'the making of peats is at best but a tiresome and tedious operation; often precarious, and attended with a heavy expence, besides the loss of the summer and autumnal months, which might be applied to much more lucrative and useful purposes'. Importing coal by sea would save a lot of time and effort. Duty on the coastal shipment of coal was removed in 1794, and after that importing coal became viable, especially when there was a return cargo. Ballachulish, for example, was provided with coal by ships which came to load slates.

Sport and Tourism

Until the late eighteenth century, the Highland landscape was seen as a problem hindering communication, rather than an attractive feature to be exploited. Then things changed, and the grandeur of the scenery came to be appreciated, and desolation seen as romantic. The minister of Kilmallie, for example, in the 1790s, described the waterfall in Glen Nevis thus: 'The appearance of this sheet of water, immediately attracts one's attention, dilates the heart, and kindles, in the mind, those lofty and grand sentiments of devotion, and those pleasing elevated feelings, which the sublime sound of a cascade, or the war of many waters, naturally excite.' James Hogg, the 'Ettrick Shepherd', in 1804 described Loch Sunart as a wild and strange scene 'being a group of precipitate rocks, green hollows and wild woods'. The geographer John Macculloch in 1824 described Loch Leven as 'one continued succession of landscapes, on both sides', particularly the lower part, 'the furthest extremity being rather wild than beautiful'. Though he did not find all scenery inspiring: 'Morvern is a mere heap of mountains, rude in character, without presenting much interest, either in their heights or their forms'.

The 1830s brought the first regular steam boats, which helped to open up the Highlands to tourism, so that by the 1890s there were complaints about the prevalence of holiday houses, with the more accessible parts of Argyll 'now occupied by long ranges of villas and cottages-ornees'. Queen Victoria in 1873 visited Glencoe, which she described as 'stern, rugged, precipitous mountains with beautiful peaks and rocks piled high one above the other, two and three thousand feet high, tower and rise up to the heavens on either side . . .' And she found 'the solemn solitude and grandeur of Glen Nevis . . . almost finer than Glencoe'.

Some visitors were happy just to observe the scenery. Others had started coming for sport. At first this was intrepid individuals who shot sea birds or fished, mainly on the islands. But during the nineteenth century country sports became more formalised. Game birds and deer became desirable prey, and the estate owners responded by organising their estates to encourage the desired animals and birds. They then either let the shooting and stalking, or enjoyed enormous patronage by entertaining friends and business or political colleagues. In 1883 the deer forests in Lochaber included Glen Quoich (33,000 acres), Ardtornish (15,000 acres), Glengarry (14,000 acres) and smaller forests at Achnacarry, Arisaig and Morar. Value was not entirely calculated in relation to size, however, and Achnacarry (6,000 acres) was valued almost as highly as Ardtornish or Glengarry. The attendant infrastructure and employment was significant.

Another new pursuit was walking or climbing for pleasure. Although there were intrepid early enthusiasts, it was the improved transport networks which brought walkers and climbers to Lochaber in far greater numbers during the nineteenth and twentieth centuries. The Ordnance Survey and others began accurately to measure the height of mountains, so that eventually Ben Nevis was recognised to be the highest (1,344 m), ousting Ben Macdui (1,309 m) from its previous pre-eminence. This brought greater numbers of climbers to

Lochaber. By 1852 the basic triangulation of Britain was complete, and over the second half of the century the maps which formed the basis for those with which we are familiar today were gradually produced.

Sir Hugh Munro, the third president of the Scottish Mountaineering Club, compiled a list of all the hills over 3,000 feet high. He published it in 1891, and himself managed to climb all but two before he died in 1919. The list originally comprised 283 peaks, though over the years as heights were remeasured the number changed slightly. Later J. Rooke Corbett compiled a list of just over 200 hills between 2,500 and 3,000 feet.

It is not known who first climbed Ben Nevis, but there were certainly those who did so in the second half of the eighteenth century who did not regard themselves as pioneering. The Scottish Mountaineering Club was founded in 1889, and the number of climbers in Lochaber increased considerably after the arrival of the West Highland Railway in 1894. In 1908 the Scottish Ladies Climbing Club was established, and in 1925 the Junior Mountaineering Club of Scotland. Junior meant not younger, but less experienced than those in the original Scottish Mountaineering Club. Those who gained experience could move up to the senior club.

Clement Wragge (1852–1922), a navigator and surveyor, met the secretary of the Scottish Meteorological Society in 1879, and offered to establish a temporary meteorological observatory at the top of Ben Nevis to prove its usefulness. He climbed the mountain every day in the summer and autumn of 1881 and 1882. He took observations at sea level and at various heights, while his wife simultaneously took observations at Fort William. As a result of his efforts, an appeal fund was established in 1883, and the Observatory (NN 166 712) was built by the Scottish Meteorological Society, being formally opened in October 1883. The Observatory had a staff of four, and was regularly supplied from Fort William. Wragge applied for the post of superintendent, but was not appointed, so he became a meteorologist in Australia. Observations were made regularly until it closed in 1904 because of lack of funds for maintenance. The low

Fig. 15. The Observatory Hotel, Ben Nevis (from an old postcard)

level observatory, on the shores of Loch Linnhe, on the edge of Fort William, built of red sandstone in 1889, also went out of use in 1904, and is now a private house (7.17) (Plate 24).

In addition to the stone-built observatory, there was also a wooden hut on the summit, used as a hostel (Fig. 15). It had accommodation for 12, and meals were served between June and September. 'Here a mountaineering enthusiast may find a comfortable night's rest, and partake of appetising fare at rates which, considering the situation, are not unreasonable'. The hostel closed in 1915. A path had been constructed to the summit, for building and supplying the observatory, and in 1911 an ascent was made in a model T Ford. This took five days.

In 1931 the Scottish Youth Hostels Association was formed, to encourage those of limited means to 'know, use and appreciate the Scottish countryside'. Its hostels include one in Glencoe. The National Trust for Scotland bought Glencoe in 1935 for £1,350, and the area has been extended by subsequent gifts.

Wartime Training Ground

The Second World War brought another change of use for some of the remoter areas. The sparse population meant that carrying out secret training was possible. The area north and west of Fort William became a restricted area, with locals and visitors needing permits to move around. Lochaber was a major centre for servicing the Atlantic convoys, and a training area for motor torpedo boats. Fort William became HMS *St Christopher*, a centre for training in the use of coastal force motor vessels. Later a naval repair base was established at Corpach. A great deal of timber was felled, and the West Highland Railway was kept busy moving men and timber, much of it shipped out through Mallaig. German bombers attacked the hydroelectric plant and aluminium factory near Fort William, but did little damage

The Irregular Warfare Special Training Centre was opened at Inverailort House (6.15) in 1940, and training was carried out over a wide area of the west coast. The Commando Basic Training Centre at Achnacarry Castle (6.1) opened in 1940, providing a twelve-week induction course for all trainees. Some 25,000 trainees came through here. It closed in early 1946. About 25,000 English, Scottish, Irish, Welsh, French, Belgian, American, Dutch and Norwegian soldiers were trained here, and it became known as 'Castle Commando'. Arisaig House (6.4) was home to the Special Operations Executive Paramilitary Training Schools.

Post-war developments

The West Highland Way was opened in 1980, partly intended to bring trade to Kinlochleven after the closure of the aluminium smelter there. Hill-walking brings many visitors to the area. There is skiing at Nevis Range and at Glencoe. At Nevis Range the ski-lifts run in summer as well, offering services to walkers and mountain cyclists, as well as spectacular views to less energetic visitors.

7. INDUSTRY

Although Lochaber does have some natural resources such as stone, coal, iron, timber and fish, there were always problems with their economic exploitation because of the limitations of geography and a population not large enough to achieve economies of scale. Only resources situated close to the coast could be realistically exploited, and only usually if there was local demand, otherwise customers could get better-quality supplies from other places. The seventeenth and eighteenth centuries saw many estate owners trying to establish industrial enterprises to enhance the profits from their estates. Usually the skilled workers needed to run such enterprises had to be imported, and many were not happy with the local living conditions, the restricted diet, the isolation or the climate. Some English capitalists took leases in order to exploit the natural resources of the Highlands, such as minerals and timber, themselves.

The York Buildings Company, whose charter allowed it unlimited powers to acquire land, bought several of the estates which had been confiscated after the Jacobite rising of 1715. On the east coast, for example, they developed the coal-works on the estate of the Earl of Winton in East Lothian, and built the first colliery waggonway in Scotland from Tranent to Cockenzie in 1722. As each venture developed difficulties, another was started with renewed optimism, but almost inevitably hit problems, in terms of the quality of the raw materials, the costs of extraction and the costs of transport. Although their main interests were elsewhere, the company did make investments in Lochaber.

Ironworks

Charcoal was the normal fuel used for processing iron. As charcoal was fragile, it made sense to locate ironworks near the sources of timber for making charcoal, even if it meant importing the iron ore. Four ironworks were established in the Highlands in the 1720s, one on Speyside, one near Loch Katrine, one at Bonawe on Loch Etive, and one at Invergarry, in Lochaber. The ironworks at Invergarry was established by William Rawlinson and partners, owners of a furnace in Lancashire. In 1727 they signed a contract with Macdonnell of Glengarry for the use of his timber. But the site was remote, and skilled labour had to be imported. The superintendent was accommodated in the old castle, on which £100 had to be spent.

The first iron was made in 1728, and customers included the York Buildings Company and General Wade. The York Buildings Company invested heavily in Invergarry in 1730, and although Rawlinson left in 1731, in 1733 a second furnace was started. But the enterprise was never a financial success, and work had stopped by 1736. The iron produced had had to be transported by land and water to a specially built quay at Corpach, adding to costs. At the same time better-quality imported Swedish iron had come down in price. The other works did not thrive either. But while they were operating they absorbed a lot of timber for making the charcoal which they used as fuel, and also exported. Bonawe is supposed to have used up all the timber from Glenuig and Roshven.

Mining

Another venture at the same date was lead-mining. In 1722 Sir Archibald Grant, General George Wade and others leased the lead-mines at Strontian (9.3), in Ardnamurchan, from Sir Alexander Murray of Stanhope, a keen mineralogist, who had bought the estates of Sunart and Ardnamurchan in 1714 because of their economic potential. In 1730 the York Buildings Company took over the lease of the mines, and spent a lot of money developing them. As well as the mines themselves, they built a quay, smelter, furnaces, hearths, a cooperage, a road and housing for the workers at a settlement they named New York, just up the valley from Strontian. Even when the mines failed, the infrastructure helped the wider development of the area, just as the military roads did. There was not enough skilled labour available locally, and some of the imported workers were unhappy at the poor local facilities. The York Buildings Company, despite the extent of its investment, failed to produce as much lead as it had predicted, and there were problems with embezzlement and speculation related to the company in general, as well as their usual over-optimistic plans. They had predicted an annual production of 10,000 tons of lead, though others felt 1,500 tons was more realistic. The most we know was shipped in any one year was 750 tons. In 1742 the company gave up its lease of the mines. They had also leased mines in Morvern and Mull, with similar lack of success.

The Strontian mines continued, however. In 1753, 60 tons of Strontian lead was used to roof the new Inveraray Castle. As well as lead, in 1764 the mineral Strontianite was discovered, and in the 1790s the chemist Thomas Hope isolated the element 'strontium', which led to a revival of the mines. The *Old Statistical Account* reported that 'there is an extensive lead work, carried on by an English company', employing about 200 men, and hoping to employ 100 more 'from the lead ores turning out beyond expectations'. The mines produced £4,000 per annum. Lead production revived during the Napoleonic Wars, due to demand for lead for bullets. The last of the mines had closed by 1871, but the twentieth century saw some mining of barytes (barium sulphate, used in some white paints), and recently work has restarted in the Whitesmith and Clashgorm areas.

There were also lead-mines at Lurga, in Liddesdale (9.2), on the opposite side of Loch Sunart. In 1733 the Morvern Mining Company had 'built a hansome dwelling house for their Manager, Clerks and Office at Liedgesdale, besides a Key with a compleat Storehouse, upon it, two Warehouses, Lodging houses for workmen, two large Stables and as many Barns, a Malt Kiln, a Smith's chop and Workhouse'. Copper ore was mined at Tearnait (9.4), on the Ardtornish estate.

Another local mine is that at Lochaline (9.5), opened in 1940 to extract silica sand, used for optical glass, when that material was no longer available from Germany. At first the sand was transported on a light railway to the west pier, where it was crushed and graded before being shipped out. More recently the processing has been done close to the mine entrance, and the mine has its own jetty at which ships can tie up while the sand is transferred into their holds along a conveyor belt.

Quarrying

At Brunachan, at the head of Glen Roy (9.7), was a quarry producing quern stones, whose products have been identified as far away as the Outer Hebrides. Many medieval churches in Mull, Morvern and Ardnamurchan incorporate dressed stone from the quarries of Inninmore Bay, on the Sound of Mull. Quarries at Inninmore (9.8) and round Loch Aline were worked until the nineteenth century, providing stone to build the Lismore lighthouse and the locks of the Crinan Canal. Between Ballachulish and Kentallen (9.9) there are granite quarries, mainly dating from the nineteenth century. Granite was also quarried around Kingairloch (9.10). Stone was quarried from the estate of Fassifern, on the north side of Loch Eil, for buildings related to the Caledonian Canal and for the first quay at Fort William. The Canal mainly got freestone from the Cumbraes, granite from Ballachulish and limestone from Lismore.

In areas where there was limestone, as for example around the shores of Loch Aline, it was burned to produce lime for use as a fertiliser and as mortar for building. Two limekilns survive there, one each side of the loch (Fig. 16). The larger one, on the west side, has an associated quay, implying it was for more than purely estate use. Other limekilns can be seen on old maps, as can many former quarries. Quarrying continues today, with Foster Yeoman's superquarry at Glensanda, one of the largest quarry operations in the world. Since 1982 it has been producing 5 million tons of granite a year, crushed for use in roads and other civil engineering projects.

Fig. 16. A small lime kiln on the east shore of Loch Aline, Morvern

The quarry has no road access, with workers being brought in by sea, and all the stone shipped out by bulk carriers.

Ballachulish (9.6) is one of the two main slate-producing areas in Scotland, the other being at Easdale just south of Oban. Slate is compacted fine-grain mud from the ancient sea bed, deposited in thin layers, along which it fractures neatly. Because it splits into thin sheets, it is useful for roofing. Different areas produce different types of slate. Welsh slate is the finest, splitting into the thinnest and most even sheets. Ballachulish slate has little pyrite crystals, which shine like brass, and are the result of the presence of iron and sulphur in the sediment. They can decay and cause holes to form.

The first quarry, at West Laroch, was opened in 1693, and East Laroch the following year. Various eighteenth-century travellers commented on the busy scene, and its contrast with the surrounding subsistence agriculture. In 1791, there were seventy-four families living there. The sheltered waters of Loch Leven made loading easy, and the slates were exported far afield. The *General View of Agriculture*, in 1794, said there were about ninety men working in the slate quarries, 'every four men, which is called a crew, are said to quarry one hundred and four thousand slates in a year, for which they receive fifteen shilling [75p] per thousand'. Slates were produced in a wide range of standard sizes. Splitting and trimming them to size was a skilled job. John Leyden, in 1800, noted that 'the workmen are chiefly from Cumberland'. Macculloch in 1824 said that 'the workmen, the noise, the shipping, the women and children, and the confusion of all kinds, form a strange contrast with the dark and dreary solitude of Glencoe itself, scarcely a mile removed'. Other visitors too commented on the noise.

By 1845 there were 300 men employed, and by 1875, 587 men, and 26 million slates were quarried and cut to shape. All work was above sea level so there were no flooding problems. 'The workings are conducted in three levels, rising above each other as steps of stairs', rising over 200 feet. Wagon-ways carried the slate down to the shore, from where it was shipped out. An inclined plane was used to carry down slate from the highest level. The harbour was formed from banks of waste slate deposited on the loch side. In the 1840s the slates were being shipped all over Scotland, and to Northumberland. Occasional cargoes were sent to America and the West Indies. The workers were accommodated in solid stone houses, built with lime mortar, and slated roofs. In 1873 Queen Victoria described the village as 'very clean and tidy – a long, continuous, straggling, winding street'.

Originally the quarries had been the property of the Stewart family, who owned the Ballachulish estate. Some time after 1780 they were let, but then reverted to family control. The family got into debt, however, trying to introduce new practices and machinery, and in 1862 the estate was sold. The new purchaser expanded production and built new houses in the village. But the property then went through a series of owners and quarry subcontractors, with several legal disputes. In 1903 there was a lock-out when the men took strike action in support of the works doctor who had been dismissed. The men won, but the Ballachulish Slate Quarries Company was dissolved, and soon afterwards the First World War led to closure for want of men, and lack of demand for slates. In 1922 work started again, in a new scheme involving worker shareholding. The quarries survived until 1955. It is possible small-scale working may start again, as the slate is in demand for the restoration of old buildings.

Kelp burning

The burning of seaweed, generally known as 'kelp', to produce an alkaline ash for use in the production of glass and soap, seems to have been introduced from Ireland to the Western Isles in the 1740s. It had been introduced slightly earlier on the east coast, but by the time prices boomed during the Napoleonic Wars it had become an important part of the economy of the west coast, where there was spare labour and a long coastline. Prices collapsed after the end of the war in 1815, reinforced by the repeal of the Salt and other Acts in 1822. By 1845 it was not worth the cost of manufacture. This created problems in Lochaber, where the land could not support the population without an extra source of income such as charcoal burning or kelp processing. It was not an ideal supplementary employment, as it was a summer job, conflicting with agricultural activities and peat cutting. On the other hand, it exploited a natural resource, its processing used unproductive land, it helped provide much-needed employment, and the finished product was easy to transport. It remained as a casual local industry in some places for the rest of the nineteenth century, and was revived on the islands later for the production of iodine from the true kelp plant, which grows below low water mark.

Many travellers reported seeing smoke from the burning of kelp in this area, and some also reported a distinctive smell. The weed, rich in potash and soda, was harvested at low tide, from the rocks. The best growth was in relatively sheltered waters, and was harvested between May and July. It was dried as quickly as possible to retain its alkali content, and stacked like hay. In some areas harvesting was organised, with defined areas cut in rotation every three years, when the new growth was highest in alkali content. The dried weed was burned in shallow 'kilns', really just stone-edged shallow pits. This was best done on a dry and windy day. The fire, using wood or heather as a fuel, was tended, the ash stirred, and more weed steadily added for about eight to ten hours, or until the 'kiln' was full. The resulting product was raked to remove impurities, then left to cool, being stirred or beaten at first to ensure an even consistency. The ash was then covered with stones to compress it and left to harden to a toffee-like consistency. When cool, after about two days, it was broken into manageable pieces and stored. A ton of kelp could be made from what can be gathered by 4 men and a boat in 2 days. The weight in a 'ton' of kelp grew from 20 to 24 hundredweight to allow for impurities. The minister of Morvern in the 1790s reported that about 70 tons was produced annually, at a cost of about 30 shillings per ton. In Kilmallie, on the other hand, little kelp was made, though the extensive coastline was exploited to harvest seaweed for manure.

Other industries

At Salen, in Ardnamurchan, a small bobbin mill was built by J. Clark of Paisley in 1840, but burned down in 1854. It used local wood supplies but in managed way.

The Ben Nevis distillery (9.14) was established near Fort William in 1823 by 'Long John' MacDonald of Keppoch. By 1908 there were three distilleries, by the 1960s only two, and today only one.

New industries in the twentieth century

In 1896 Fort William became the first town in Britain to be lit by hydroelectricity, supplied by the Lochaber Power Scheme to the Fort William Electric Lighting Company.

In 1894, advised by Lord Kelvin, the British Aluminium Company acquired rights to establish an aluminium smelting works at Kinlochleven, but only started building in 1906 (9.13). The works opened in 1909, and were extended in the 1930s. They were one of

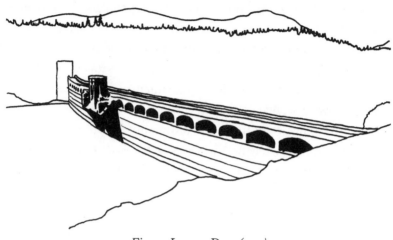

Fig. 17. Laggan Dam (9.12)

the last such enterprises to be constructed using manpower alone. The plant was powered by water from the Blackwater Reservoir on Rannoch Moor. Work at the Blackwaterfoot Dam was hard and lonely, and there were many casualties. The end of Loch Leven was dredged and a new pier built. Aluminium was in great demand during the First World War, so 1,200 German prisoners were brought in to improve the water catchment, and they also built a road.

Before the coming of the aluminium works there were few buildings at the head of Loch Leven. There was an inn (later incorporated into the Tartan Hotel, and destroyed by a flood in 1962). Other buildings included a corn mill, and a short-lived lint mill. With the coming of the aluminium works a town rapidly grew up. The works has now closed, though there is still a power station, and there is a visitor centre explaining the story of aluminium processing in the Highlands.

A second aluminium smelting plant was established at Inverlochy in 1928 (9.11), with water provided by damming Loch Treig, and building a fifteen-mile-long tunnel to convey the water to the plant. Additional water was provided in 1933 from a long curved concrete dam at the west end of Loch Laggan (9.12) (Fig. 17), and the supply further boosted in 1944. British Alcan is a major landowner in the

Lochaber area, and Inverlochy Mains Farm became the British Aluminium Club in the 1960s. Aluminium was in high demand during the Second World War as it was used for the construction of aeroplanes.

At Annat Point, Corpach, a pulp and paper mill was built 1963–6 by Wiggins Teape, at a cost of £20 million, to process Forestry Commission wood. The only integrated pulp and paper mill in UK, it was sited here because of the availability of timber, lots of fresh water, and tidal water to disperse waste water and for ease of transport. There were also good road and rail links. But, like many such industrial enterprises encouraged to set up in areas of high unemployment but with the initiative not coming from within the area, it was not a success, and the pulp mill closed in 1981, though the paper mill still functions on the site.

Today the economy of Lochaber is based on numerous smaller industries rather than a few large ones. The major employers are tourism, service industries, forestry and fish-farming. Fort William now has a supermarket, and outlets for several national retail chains.

8. COMMUNICATIONS

Let no man imagine that he understands the true nature of patience, till he has made a Highland tour, on Highland ponies, and in Highland boats. (John Macculloch, 1824)

Maritime communications

The earliest prehistoric communities in Scotland, the mesolithic hunter-gatherers, almost certainly used simple boats, as they settled on islands, and appear to have caught fish which live in relatively deep waters. Such boats were probably made either of animal skins stretched over a framework of wood, or from a hollowed-out tree trunk. Both the Picts and the Gaelic rulers of Argyll clearly used the sea for communication, and occasionally for warfare. And the Dalriadans had trade links with the rest of Britain, Gaul and perhaps further afield. Their boats may have been of wood, like the Viking longships, or may have been of skin on a wooden framework, like the Irish curragh. There are very few depictions of boats from the Dark Ages, but Pictish ones seem to have been double-ended and to have had masts. And the Vikings certainly used boats. The descendants of their oared sailing ships, the west highland galleys, continued in use until the eighteenth century. They are depicted on some late-medieval graveslabs (Plate 6), and feature on the banners of most clan chiefs.

Being part of a maritime culture meant not just owning boats, but being visited by them. Many vessels travelled from northern Europe to southern Europe and beyond by the northabout route, and the northern and western isles and the western parts of the mainland were often visited by ships. There is an account in 1622 of the problem of drunkenness in the Western Isles. It seems that when a ship carrying wine called in, an orgy resulted, often leading to breach of the peace. In other words, the supply of French wine to the Western Isles may well have been quicker and cheaper, and certainly more direct, in 1622 than it is today.

In the reprisals after Culloden some of the coastal lands of Lochaber were deliberately burned, and the navy had specific orders to destroy boats. This must have meant the loss of the local boatbuilding tradition, and there is evidence that after that date some boats were imported, sometimes in kit form, from Norway. Most local boats after that date were certainly small and simple. John Knox, writing in 1786 'observed a number of Highland boats, with four oars, and containing, generally, six or seven men', between the mainland and Skye. He also noted that 'they sing in chorus, observing a kind of time, with the movement of the oars'. He heard either singing or piping from 'almost every boat' on his travels. Other travellers made similar comments.

In the 1790s the parish of Kilmallie had eighty to a hundred boats, sixty of them based at Maryburgh (Fort William). There were also a few larger ships, four sloops (20 to 40 tons) and one brig (200 tons). These were used to import meal, flour, oats, butter, cheese, whisky (c.15,000 gallons a year, at 4 sh. [20p] per gallon), foreign spirits, salt, timber, tar and all kinds of mercantile goods. Exports included fish, wool, sheep, horses and black cattle. Wool was mostly sent to Liverpool and other English ports. There were eight ferries, five across salt water and three across fresh. In Ardnamurchan, for a population of 4,542, there were 183 small boats and five 'small vessels'. Morvern had about a hundred small boats for fishing, and for carrying seaweed for manure, 'also 12 or 14 barges of a larger size, well rigged, the property of the gentlemen tacksmen, for transporting themselves occasionally to the neighbouring islands, and for other purposes of usefulness and convenience'. In addition, there was one coasting vessel of about twenty tons.

Bowman, touring in 1826–7, on arrival at Fort William, was

'paddled ashore in a coble or coracle, more oblong than those which may still be seen on the rivers of Wales'. He commented that 'these frail and precarious barks' had been around for 200 years, except that hide was now 'substituted by canvas strongly pitched [covered with tar]'. Boat-users could be ambitious. The minister of Ardnamurchan in 1838 described how open boats from the Western Isles were in the practice of entering Loch Shiel by the river, 'and taking away ladings of the timber on its banks'. Some fishermen used a double portage, crossing from Loch Eil to Loch Shiel, then down the river to the sea. Ardnamurchan in the 1830s had two decked vessels of fifty and twenty tons, ten to twelve sailing boats of between three and eight tons, and 'innumerable row boats, almost every family possessing one'.

The middle classes used boats or horses until the building of roads for wheeled traffic, which in many places did not happen until the second half of the nineteenth century. Norman Macleod remembered the boat used by his grandfather: 'The minister's boat was about eighteen feet keel, undecked, and rigged fore and aft'. The lairds also had 'their handsome 'barge', or well-built, well-rigged 'smack' or 'wherry'; and their stately piper, who played pibrochs . . . from the bow of the boat, with the tartan ribbands fluttering from the grand war-pipe, spread the news of the chief's arrival for miles across the water'. Some landowners in the first half of the nineteenth century built boathouses in which to keep such boats (Fig. 18). A visitor to Morvern described how 'people travelled very much in their own sailing boats from place to place. Indeed there was no house of any pretensions without its boathouse. It was as necessary as stables, and more so'.

The minister of Morvern in the 1790s had lamented the need for better and more regular transport links with centres of population. Ferries were irregular: 'though the boatmen ferry at times, one cannot force them out but when it suits their humour and conveniency, and even then at whatever rates they please to exact'. Steam boats were introduced from the 1820s, though it was the middle of the

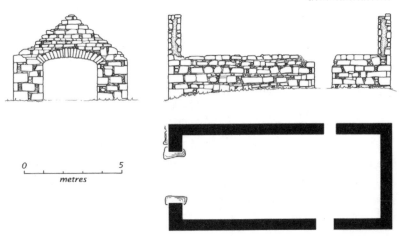

0 ————— 5
metres

Fig 18. Plan and elevations of the early nineteenth century boathouse at Fiunary, Morvern (Colin Martin) (10.11)

century before they became really reliable. By 1821 there was a Glasgow to Tobermory steamer service. The *Comet* began a regular service between Glasgow and Fort William. When the Caledonian Canal was opened in 1822 a through service began from Glasgow to Inverness. The Fort William Steamboat Company was established in 1824 (Fig. 19). In 1850 the business was taken over by its rival, Messrs Burns & Co, with the *Cygnet* and the *Lapwing*. They then sold out to David Hutcheson, who according to Joseph Mitchell owned 'a splendid fleet of steamers now navigating the intricacies of the Hebrides, the West coast of Scotland, and the Caledonian Canal'. When he died in 1881 the services continued under his junior partner David MacBrayne. By the late nineteenth century there were regular steamer links with Glasgow and Inverness. The weekly boat to Glasgow continued until 1974. There were steamer services on the large inland lochs as well. The *Clanranald I* and *Clanranald II* steam launches, for example, served in Loch Shiel from 1899 to 1953, carrying goods, passengers and mail, though the *Clanranald II* was converted to diesel in 1936.

Sea transport has its drawbacks. M.E.M. Donaldson in 1920

Fig. 19. View of Fort William with a paddle-steamer at the pier (from Anon, Mountain Moor and Loch, 1894)

described getting off the ferry from Oban at Kilchoan, which involved transferring to a smaller boat:

> This is often, in more ways than one, a veritable Noah's Ark, something of everything being thrown into it, and on top of all, the mails ... Though the ferryman is as skilful as he is courteous, genial, and invariably good-tempered, it is in rough weather sometimes a risky and Herculean labour getting the ferry-boat to the landing slip.

At low tide, a horse and cart were backed into the water and cargo and passengers unloaded into it. Even when a pier was built at Kilchoan, it was not usable at low tide. Unless a full boatload could be arranged, animals for sale at Oban therefore had to be walked fifty-four miles to Lochaline for shipment. She claimed that 'Macbrayne exercise what amounts practically to a despotic monarchy in the Western Highlands, and treat the public as they please'. She claimed that freight cost 30 shillings [£1.50] per ton from Bombay to Glasgow, and £4 per ton from Glasgow to Kilchoan.

Ferries of all sizes operated at various times, dependent on population centres, and industrial or agricultural activities. At least three are recorded along the length of Loch Sunart, for example. The main ones were associated with 'change houses', places not grand enough for the title 'inn'. Gradually in the twentieth century ferries have been replaced by bridges wherever possible, and roll-on-roll-off vessels introduced where they are still essential. There used to be a ferry for seven miles along the coast from Lochailort to Glenuig until a road was built in 1968. The Ballachulish ferry (10.6), a very old crossing point, carried its first car in 1906, driven on to two planks laid across an open boat, which was rowed across. In 1912 two motor boats with turntables were introduced, each carrying one car. A new boat in 1926 could carry two cars. By 1948 there were two ferries each carrying six cars. As the number of cars increased, long queues often built up. The number of cars wanting to cross increased nearly fivefold between 1954 and 1974, and in 1975 the ferry was replace by a bridge. The Corran ferry (10.7) has been important from the fifteenth century or earlier, as it lay on a cattle-droving route from Morvern and Ardnamurchan to Glencoe and on into Central Scotland. Originally slightly to the north, it moved to its present position when steam boats with turntables were introduced. The ferry rights belonged to the Macleans of Ardgour until the 1930s, when they handed them over to Argyll County Council. By the 1950s, the ferry could hold four or five cars. The newest ferry, *Corran*, can carry up to thirty. Other ferries which still survive include Camusnagael to Fort William, Drimnin and Loch Sunart to Tobermory (Mull), Kilchoan to Tobermory, Lochaline to Fishnish (Mull), Mallaig to Armadale (Skye), Mallaig to Eigg, Muck, Rum and Canna, and Mallaig to Loch Nevis. And although a pleasure trip rather than a ferry, the only way to travel the length of Loch Shiel is by boat.

There were inevitably accidents at sea. Perhaps the most famous in this area is when the steamer *Stirling Castle* was wrecked at Inverscaddle, north of Ardgour, in 1828. Colonel Alexander Ranaldson Macdonell, chief of Glengarry, tried to jump clear onto the rocks, but slipped and hit his head and died. The only lifeboat in Lochaber is the one which has been based at Mallaig since 1948. Neighbouring stations include Oban, Tobermory, Barra and Portree.

A writer in the 1880s said 'what we wish to impress upon the tourist is, that if he is thoroughly to appreciate and enjoy the West

Highlands, he must, if he is wise, be frequently afloat, paddling his own canoe, or having somebody else paddling it for him'. Today there are pleasure trips for tourists on sea and lochs, and the opportunity to charter boats designed for fishing or diving. Sailing and diving both bring in many visitors, and are important additions to the economy of Lochaber. Canoeing, both around the coast and on the turbulent rivers is also popular. Water transport is a good way to reach isolated places, and provides opportunities for observing wildlife, both marine and terrestrial.

Caledonian Canal

Links to Inverness were greatly improved by the Caledonian Canal (10.15–10.20), described by Queen Victoria as 'a very wonderful piece of engineering', though she added that 'travelling by it is very tedious'. The scheme was one of several designed to provide employment in the area after the Forty-Five. In 1773 James Watt did a survey and prepared designs, commissioned by the Trustees of the Forfeited Estates, but the plans were too ambitious and expensive. In 1793 plans by Rennie were also rejected on grounds of cost. Then during the war with France the Canal moved up the agenda as it would prove useful to protect shipping from French privateers off the north-east coast, while the work might help to stem the flow of emigrants. Telford did a survey in 1801–2, and an Act of Parliament was passed in 1803. Most canals were built by private enterprise, but the Caledonian Canal was perhaps the first nationalised enterprise, as the government not only paid for the construction, but took permanent responsibility for its maintenance.

The estimated cost was £350,000, and the estimated time for building seven years. The cost rapidly rose to £474,000 because of land purchase and compensation. Some lairds were hostile, fearing loss of local control. There was a long dispute with Glengarry (the larger-than-life, and difficult-to deal-with Glengarry who died in a shipwreck in 1828) about compensation for land, and rights on Loch

Oich. Work began at both ends in 1804, but costs mounted because the Napoleonic Wars raised the price of both labour and materials. All available oak was needed for the navy, so the lock gates had to be made of pine sheathed with iron. By 1805 the Canal project was employing 900 men. In 1806 Loch Oich was dredged to deepen it, with great difficulty, as it was full of sunken tree trunks. In 1822 the Canal was opened, though it was only two-thirds complete. It had to be closed after flood damage in 1834. Further work to finish it was carried out between 1843 and 1847. By May 1849 the project had cost £1,311,270, about three times the original estimate.

The highest point of the Canal, Loch Oich, is 105 feet above sea level. A reservoir was constructed in Glen Garry to provide water to keep the depth up. The water level in Loch Lochy was raised nine feet above its natural level. There are twenty-eight locks, fourteen each side of Loch Oich. The lochs themselves account for forty-five miles, with only twenty-two miles of canal. The plan had been to make the canal deep enough to accommodate 32-gun frigates as well as commercial vessels, but this proved overambitious. When first opened the canal could only take ships of less than twelve-feet draught. It was planned to be 110 feet (33 m) wide at the top, 50 feet (15 m) wide at the bottom and 20 feet (6 m) deep. However, this was difficult to achieve, and even after it was fully completed in 1847 the shallowest part was only seventeen feet (5 m) deep.

There was a tow-path along the canal sections, but boats were expected to sail along the lochs. Given the prevailing wind, this was not always easy, and later steam tugs were introduced. Dues were charged, but they did not cover the cost of maintenance. It was saved from being a white elephant by the advent of steamboats, and the regular traffic they provided. The canal 'has never answered well the grand design for which it was formed, of carrying sea-borne vessels from sea to sea along Glenmore'. But although it never carried the commercial traffic which had originally been envisaged, it was well used by fishing boats. In 1870, when large shoals of herring were reported in the Minch, 512 fishing boats came through the canal. It has also needed frequent maintenance. In the 1960s and '70s all the lock gates were replaced. The 1970s also saw the beginning of the hiring of pleasure cruisers, a business which proved very popular. As fishing traffic has declined, pleasure traffic has taken its place, and the smaller boats cause less wear and tear than the large ones the canal was built for.

The work of building it, however, provided employment, both directly and indirectly, and helped to open up the area. Fir, birch and ash were supplied from Glengarry and the estates of Locheil, floated down to a sawmill where the river Loy met the river Lochy. Locheil provided slate from a quarry at North Ballachulish, and a quarry was opened at Fassifern on Loch Eil, though some stone had to come from further afield by sea, including limestone from Lismore.

There was another, unfulfilled, scheme for a canal from Loch Eil to Loch Shiel and out to the sea, allowing ships to bypass Ardnamurchan Point, where 'the sea rises with the abrupt and irregular motion occasioned by storm tides, so very dangerous to open boats'. But like many such schemes it came to nothing. As shipping on the west coast increased, a lighthouse was built on Ardnamurchan Point in 1846–9. Designed by Alan Stevenson, who also designed the Skerryvore light (1844), it was constructed of granite from Mull. The same firm also built the little lighthouse at the Corran Narrows in 1860 (10.14).

Roads and bridges

Roads came late to the west Highlands because, as one writer in the *Old Statistical Account* put it, 'the convenience of water carriage, exempts the people . . . from the absolute necessity of an expensive attention to the roads'. Before the eighteenth century there were two main types of roads – drove roads and coffin roads. Drove roads were the traditional routes along which cattle were walked (and swum across intervening stretches of water) to markets in central Scotland, mainly Crieff and Falkirk. There were intermediate cattle markets on the droving routes, including ones at Strontian and Duror. There were also established places where cattle could rest and feed. One such is at Larmachfoldach, on the old road from Fort William to Kinlochleven. Cattle from islands such as Barra, for example, would be landed at McNeil's Bay, near the Ardnamurchan lighthouse, or at Kilchoan, and then walked on. Some cattle from Morvern were ferried across to Mull. Another route ran east from Skye by various trails, most converging on Wade's High Bridge over the Spean. Other routes converged on Rannoch Moor, heading towards Loch Earn. Droving increased during the eighteenth century, because of the demand created by the fast-growing cities, and the needs of the army and navy.

Coffin roads led to remote graveyards, and particularly to the traditional burial isles. St Finan's Isle, in Loch Shiel (3.10), was approached by several roads from all directions, including, for example, a road from Strontian northwards over the hill via Beallach nan Carn to Pollach, from where the coffin would be taken the last section by boat. Another ran over the south shoulder of Ben Resipol. And there was a coffin road between Loch Lochy and Loch Garry.

Such goods as had to be transported overland were carried by packmen or on pack ponies. As Norman Macleod remembered, 'one of the most welcome visitors was the packman', carrying 'a choice selection of everything which a family was likely to require from the lowland shops . . . Ribbons, like rainbows, were unrolled; prints held up in graceful folds before the light; cheap shawls were displayed on the back of some handsome lass, who served as a model . . . the news, gathered on his travels, was as welcome to the minister as his goods were to his family'. The post was brought by a 'runner', who was in fact 'a sedate walker'.

Had you seen these roads before they were made,
You'd have held up your hands and bless'd General Wade.

General George Wade (1673–1748) was appointed Commander-in Chief in Scotland in 1724. It was obvious to him that he could not move soldiers around or get supplies to forts unless he had roads. So he started to build them, using soldiers but also some civilians. In the words of Thomas Pennant in 1769, 'like another Hannibal', Wade 'forced his way through rocks supposed to have been unconquerable', using gunpowder where necessary. Between 1725 and 1733 he built nearly 250 miles of road, theoretically of a standard width of sixteen feet (4.9 m). At first rivers were forded, but later he went back and built bridges where they were needed. The only Wade road in Lochaber is the southern section of the Great Glen Road from Fort William to Inverness, built between 1725 and 1727. It includes two major bridges, High Bridge across Glen Spean (10.24) (Plate 13), and Low Bridge across Glen Gloy (10.25).

In the aftermath of the 1745 rebellion, the road-building programme was restarted in 1750, under Major William Caulfield. His roads were more sophisticated, with more cuttings and embankments. In this area is the north end of his road from Stirling to Fort William, coming from the top of Glencoe over the Devil's Staircase to Kinlochleven, and then over the Lairaig Mhor and down Glen Nevis. In 1786 this was replaced by a new road from Glencoe to Fort William via Onich, but parts of the old road are now incorporated in the West Highland Way.

Military road-building stopped in the 1770s, and without maintenance many roads gradually deteriorated. The minister of Kilmallie in the 1790s reported that bridges and government roads were good, but the county roads poor and 'much neglected'. There were two four-wheeled chaises in the parish, one belonging to a vintner in Fort William, and the other for hire. There were also three two-wheeled vehicles and about two dozen carts. 'Sledges are chiefly used in leading home hay and corn. Peats, for the most part, are carried in creels upon horseback'. The minister of Morvern reported that the road along the shores of the Sound of Mull, kept up by statute labour, was 'for the most part rideable'. Roads in the rest of parish were very poor. 'The people, however, are now becoming more sensible of the advantages that would arise from

1. Clach-a-Charra standing stone, Onich (1.9). (Colin Martin)

2. One of the kerb cairns at Claggan, Morvern (1.1). (Colin Martin)

3. Free-standing cross, Iona School, fourteenth–fifteenth century, Kiel, Morvern (3.3). (Colin Martin)

4. Lower part of another cross depicting a bishop, Iona School, fourteenth–fifteenth century, Kiel, Morvern (3.3). (Colin Martin)

5. *An arch from the medieval church at Kiel, Morvern, surviving in the graveyard (3.3). (Paula Martin)*

6. *A West Highland galley – detail from a late-medieval grave slab, Kiel, Morvern (3.3). (Colin Martin)*

7. Cill Choirille (St Cyril), Glen Spean (3.2). (Colin Martin)

8. Relocated gate from the fort at Fort William, 1690 (5.8). (Paula Martin)

9. Inverlochy Castle (4.7). (Colin Martin)

10. Castle Tioram, Moidart (4.11). (Colin Martin)

11. Eilean Munde, burial isle in Loch Leven (3.11). (Colin Martin)

12. Gravestone on Eilean Munde commemorating a man who killed a dragoon at Prestonpans in 1745 (3.11). (Colin Martin)

13. High Bridge, 1736–7 (10.24). (Colin Martin)

14. Glenfinnan Monument (12.5). (Colin Martin)

15. Kingshouse, Glencoe (10.45). (Colin Martin)

16. Parliamentary Church, Acharacle, 1829–33 (5.1). (Paula Martin)

17. Nineteenth-century coffin cairns (10.22). (Colin Martin)

18. Ardnamurchan Parish Church, Kilchoan, 1827–31 (5.22). (Paula Martin)

19. Cleared strip of beach in front of a ruined cottage, Camas nan Geall, Ardnamurchan (8.20). (Paula Martin)

20. Fish trap, near Kingairloch (8.16). (Colin Martin)

21. Ardtornish House, with its boathouse in the foreground (6.3). (Colin Martin)

22. Inverlochy Castle Hotel (4.7). (Paula Martin)

23. Dalelia, Loch Shiel (6.8). (Paula Martin)

24. Low-level Weather Observatory, Fort William (7.17). (Paula Martin)

25. Kinlochmoidart Pier, a typical steamer pier (10.4). (Paula Martin)

26. Pair of concrete cottages, Inninbeg, Ardtornish estate, Morvern, 1879 (8.2). (Paula Martin)

27. *Glenfinnan Railway Viaduct, 1897–1901 (10.35). (Colin Martin)*

28. *Concrete bridge, Glencoe, 1930s (10.33). (Colin Martin)*

29. Commando Monument, Spean Bridge (12.8). (Colin Martin)

good roads', but progress was slow because so few of the landowners were resident, and because of the number of streams to be crossed. There were only three bridges, and one of them was ruinous. Travel was uncomfortable. Joseph Mitchell (1803–83) contrasted his experiences with those of his father, 'traversing the country when there were no roads of any kind, crossing dangerous rivers and streams, travelling in wet clothes, and for shelter living in smoky and wretched huts, where oat cakes, milk and whisky were the chief or only refreshments'.

In 1803 Parliament appointed two Commissioners for Highland Roads and Bridges, with Thomas Telford (already the official engineer to the Scottish Fisheries Society) as their engineer, and between 1803 and 1823 he laid the basis of the modern road network. The cost of these new roads, the first to be designed for wheeled traffic, was to be shared with local landowners. These Parliamentary roads included Fort William to Arisaig (finished 1812), complete with post office and inn at Arisaig (Fig. 20); Invergarry to Kinloch Hourn (finished 1812); and Corran Ferry to Kinlochmoidart via the head of Loch Sunart. This included piers at both sides of the Corran Ferry, intended for cattle rather than for foot passengers or vehicles. In 1814 the Commissioners took over responsibility for the former military roads. A new road from Spean Bridge via Loch Laggan and Kingussie replaced the Wade road over the Corrieairack Pass. Telford roads were supposed to be sixteen feet (4.88 m) wide to allow two coaches or carts to pass, though where they had to be cut through rock, or at bridges, they narrowed to twelve feet (3.66 m). There are many minor single-track roads in the area today which are barely ten feet (3 m) wide. Wherever possible the gradient was no steeper than 1 in 30. An inspector was appointed to check the building and repair of these new roads. This was first John Mitchell then, from 1824 to 1863, his son Joseph, whose memoirs survive, published in 1883. He covered an average of 9,500 miles each year. Telford took on no new contracts after 1816, and his road building finished in 1821, but it had employed an average of 2,700 men. From 1813 the Commissioners for

Fig. 20. The inn and post office built at Arisaig at the same time as the Parliamentary Road, c.1810 (10.39)

Highland Roads and Bridges did award annual grants for repairs, to be topped up with local contributions.

Road building in the Highlands was difficult. Knox in 1786 noted that 'the roads which are carried along the sides of the mountains, require to be guarded from the numerous little torrents that pour from above, in wet weather . . .', and the engineering and cost involved was beyond the capability of most landowners. Once the example was set by central government, however, some roads were eventually taken on by consortia of landowners. The road along Glen Nevis, for example, was built to provide work during the potato famine in 1846. But the trouble with making better roads is that they get used more heavily, leading to increased wear and tear, and therefore increased maintenance costs. This was demonstrated long ago, but still takes people by surprise today.

The Roads Commission was wound up in 1862 because the Highlands were now sufficiently prosperous. But it was only in

Fig. 21. A cast-iron milepost, Ardnamurchan

the 1860s that the network of roads began to approach the modern pattern. In the 1840s the minister of Morvern could still write that 'there are as yet no roads'. By the 1820s more commercial travellers were using gigs rather than horses, and the number of such travellers was increasing. Increasing commerce meant that a formal road system was increasingly necessary. The minister of Ardnamurchan in 1838 commented that ten years before there had been no carts in the parish, but now they were 'not uncommon'. The postal network improved, and post offices were established in the main centres of population. By 1838, for example, there were post offices in Strontian, Kilchoan and Arisaig.

Stage coaches were run to Fort William from Glasgow and Inverness. Once the Highland Railway (Perth to Inverness) opened in 1864, coaches from Fort William linked to it at Kingussie. A number of attractive cast-iron mileposts mark roads laid out or improved during the later nineteenth century (Fig. 21). The twentieth century has seen the building of new roads and the re-routing, straightening and widening of existing ones. The road along the south side of Loch Leven was built by German prisoners during the First World War. The new road from Bridge of Orchy to Ballachulish, through

Glencoe, was built in 1933 (the old road ran the other side of Loch Tulla). From 1966 the road from the Corran Ferry which had stopped abruptly in Moidart was extended from Glenuig to Lochailort, so joining the road from Fort William to Mallaig.

Bridges

High Bridge (Plate 13), about three miles west of Spean Bridge, was built in 1736 by General Wade, over the gorge of the Spean, at a cost of £1,087. Most of the bridges built on military roads, however, were quite small, and did not satisfy the needs of cattle drovers. Telford built larger, solider bridges on his Parliamentary roads, but this was expensive, as they averaged two per mile in this area. There was a lack of skilled and experienced road contractors, and the government therefore required that roads had to be maintained by the builder for the first three years. Everyone, even Telford, underestimated the power of winter spates, and there were many disasters with roads and bridges washed away, particularly in 1818.

Bridge building has continued ever since, both replacing early bridges with wider ones, and gradually replacing fords and ferry crossings with bridges. The river Lochy, north of Fort William, was first bridged in 1849. This bridge was replaced in 1929 and again in 1965. When the road through Glencoe was improved in the 1930s two very distinctive concrete bridges were also constructed (Plate 28). The Ballachulish ferry was replaced by a bridge in 1975.

Inns and Hotels

Up to the end of the eighteenth century most inns were primitive. Keeping an inn was a part-time job, combined with farming, smuggling, and illegal distilling. Inns or 'change houses' were situated at intervals along main roads, and at ferry points. In 1800 John Leyden stayed at the inn at Strontian, still called the 'London House, having been originally constructed of wood in that city and conveyed to Strontian in a ship. The accommodation is very bad, as may be expected. The floor of my bedroom was rotten and full of large holes ... the panes of the window were shattered; and I discovered in the morning that an unlucky breeze had blown my night-cap from my head and scattered my clothes on the floor'.

With the Parliamentary roads came better inns. The inn at Arisaig was established as soon as the Parliamentary road from Fort William was recommended to be built. Inns are rarely mentioned in the *Old Statistical Account*, though there were two in Fort William. The *Second Statistical Account*, however, published in 1845, often lists them. By this time there were three in Fort William, and others at Ardgour, Arisaig, Clachaig (Glencoe), Duror, Glenfinnan and Strontian. Other inns with a long history include the King's House at the top of Glencoe (Plate 15) and the Glenuig Inn.

During the second half of the nineteenth century hotels as we know them developed, some built on long-established inn sites, and some on new sites. Perhaps the finest local example of a 'Highland Hotel' is the Ballachulish Hotel. A surprisingly large number of Victorian and Edwardian hotels, however, have been destroyed by fire. The Banavie Hotel, for example, built in 1848 and enlarged in the 1880s, burned down in 1924 and was demolished. Torcastle house, converted to a hotel in 1947, burned down in 1950. Horseley Hall, later the Loch Sunart Hotel, burned down in the late 1990s. By contrast the Tartan Hotel at Kinlochleven, an extended eighteenth century inn, was washed away when the river Leven flooded in 1962.

Railways

What revolutionised the landscape, and opened it up to tourists and sportsmen, was the coming of the railways. Roads had had a considerable impact, as had the Caledonian Canal, but nothing compared to the effect of the railways. One of the last of these was the West Highland Line, opened from Glasgow to Fort William in 1894, and on to Mallaig in 1901 (Fig. 22). Queen Victoria had

Fig. 22. A train on the West Highland Railway (after Anon., Mountain Moor and Loch, *1894)*

bought Balmoral Castle in 1848, and holidaying in the Highlands was given the royal seal of approval. Those with holiday homes in Lochaber included Lord Strathcona, who made his money in the Hudson Bay Company and the Canadian Pacific Railway (Glencoe), Octavius Smith, a London brewer (Ardtornish), Robert Stewart of Ingliston, brewer (Kinlochmoidart), and Professor Hugh Blackburn of Glasgow University (Roshven). His wife Jemima painted charming watercolours which give a vivid picture of a comfortable but adventurous outdoor life, with many distinguished guests.

In 1884 the Glasgow and North Western Railway, backed by the North British Railway, was formed to build a line from Glasgow to Fort William via Strathblane, the east side of Loch Lomond, Crianlarich, and Rannoch Moor, to cross Loch Leven at Ballachulish and then follow the coast to Fort William. It was planned to carry on up the Great Glen to join the Highland Railway just south of Inverness. This would have reduced the distance by rail between Glasgow and Inverness by forty-seven miles. But the Highland Railway managed to get the Bill defeated. Three years late the project was revived, but just for a line from Helensburgh to Fort William, this time approaching Fort William via Spean Bridge, and dropping the proposal to continue on up the Great Glen. A proposal to carry it on to Roshven, five miles short of Mallaig, was dropped because of opposition from landowners. The Act of Parliament was passed on 12 August 1889, followed by agreement for another short stretch to link Fort William to Banavie, on the Caledonian Canal. Its length was to be 100 miles.

The first turf was cut in Fort William in October 1889, and work started at Helensburgh, Arrochar, Crianlarich and Tyndrum. The complete line was opened to passenger traffic on 7 August 1894, with a formal opening a few days later, when 250 guests who had travelled from Glasgow were welcomed in Fort William by cheering crowds and a triumphal arch made from heather, and treated to dinner and speeches. The return trip took five and a half hours. In 1895 the extension to Banavie opened, and a Bill was introduced to extend that line to Mallaig. The Highland Railway, which had plans for a line to Kyle of Lochalsh, opposed the scheme, but eventually a compromise was reached, in which the West Highland and North British Companies would not make plans for a line through the Great Glen for ten years. In 1896 the Act was passed for the Mallaig line and the building of a harbour at Mallaig. The government backed the project with financial guarantees in the hope of developing the fishing industry, and the line opened on 1 April 1901.

Various companies had plans to build a railway along the Great Glen. The North British wanted to build northwards from Fort William to Inverness, while the Highland Railway wanted to do it from Inverness southwards. The railway had also reached Oban in 1880, and the Caledonian Railway proposed building a line from Oban via Ballachulish and Fort William to Inverness. The only line ever built in the Great Glen ran from Spean Bridge to Fort Augustus, and was opened in 1903 (from Fort Augustus one took a boat along Loch Ness to Inverness). But the Invergarry and Fort Augustus Railway spent so much money on the engineering of the track that there was none left for rolling-stock, and the Highland Railway took over the running of the line, which closed in 1933, re-opened, then closed again in 1946. Remains can still be seen between Spean Bridge and Fort Augustus. A tunnel was built so that the residents of Glengarry Castle would not be disturbed by the trains. The station at Invergarry also had to have an extra-large canopy to keep important guests dry as they left the train.

Meanwhile the Caledonian Railway was still planning a line from Oban to Ballachulish, while the North British planned a line from Fort William to the Corran Narrows. The Ballachulish slate quarries wanted the line, but the Aluminium works at Kinlochleven insisted that the bridge across the mouth of Loch Leven should be high enough to allow ships underneath. The line from Oban to Ballachulish opened in 1903, with bridges at Connel and Creagan. But it never got further than Ballachulish, and was closed in 1966.

9. Lochaber in Literature, Art and Music

Language

According to the minister of Kilmallie in the 1790s, the locals spoke a very pure form of Gaelic, but 'there are very few people, especially of the younger class, who do not understand and speak English. It is remarkable, yet not the less true, that the illiterate Highlander, who is a stranger to every other language but the Gaelic, speaks it more fluently, more elegantly, and more purely, than the scholar'. This view was echoed by other ministers. By the 1840s the ministers were commenting that English was more widely understood, and put this down mainly to the opening up of communications with the south by steamboats. In the remoter areas such changes had been dramatic. According to one minister in 1836 travel had opened minds and 'we have learned that there is a world beyond Glenelg'.

The eighteenth century saw Gaelic culture moving into print. The original remit of the Highland Society of Scotland, established in 1784, had included 'the preservation of the language, poetry, and music of the Highlands', although they soon concentrated on agricultural improvement. They set up a committee after the death of Macpherson in 1796 to enquire into the authenticity of Ossian. Its report was finally published in 1805. After this they decided to produce a Gaelic dictionary, which eventually appeared in 1828.

Literature in Lochaber

Ossian, the legendary Gaelic bard, son of Fingal, is said to have been born in Glencoe in the third century AD. In 1763 the scholar James Macpherson (1736–96) published *Temora*, an epic in eight books which claimed to be a translation of the work of Ossian. Many people were taken in, though there were also many sceptics, including Dr Samuel Johnson. After Macpherson's death it was found that although his work was not a total fake, being based on traditional Gaelic tales and oral sources, he had made additions and alterations of his own in order to reinterpret the Gaelic past for the tastes of a more genteel Enlightenment Scotland. The supposed works of Ossian were translated into Italian (1763), German (1764) and French (1774). Whatever the merits or otherwise of Macpherson, the interest in Ossian helped to bring travellers to the Highlands.

Iain Lom (John MacDonald) (*c.*1625–after 1707), the bard of the MacDonalds of Keppoch, was well-educated, having spent several years at a seminary. A poet and warrior, described as an 'uncompromising Catholic', and by another source as a 'frensied Jacobite', he was a follower of Montrose. His best-known poem is *The Battle of Inverlochy*, describing Montrose's victory over Argyll in 1645. He was present, and is said to have been the person who overtook Montrose at Fort Augustus and told him that Argyll was at Inverlochy, 'and thus indirectly the cause of one of the completest victories ever gained by Montrose'. He was also present at Killiecrankie in 1649. His work provides a vivid first-hand account of the rivalries between the Campbells and the MacDonalds, as well as national events. An ardent Royalist, Iain Lom is probably the author of a work hostile to the Act of Union in 1707. Although he cannot be proved to be the author, there are no other obvious candidates.

At the Restoration, Charles II appointed him the first (and only) Gaelic Poet Laureate. He never married, and died around 1709. He is buried in Cill Choirille churchyard, and is commemorated by a Victorian monument near the church door, erected 'through the munificence and patriotism of Mr Fraser Mackintosh of Drummond, MP'. His poetry was 'rough and rugged' but good and popular. Perhaps his most famous poem is the address to Sir James MacDonald of Sleat's birlinn (war galley). His walking stick is in the West Highland Museum.

There was a group of female Gaelic poets in the late seventeenth and early eighteenth centuries, including Sileas na Ceapaich (Cicely MacDonald of Keppoch).

Perhaps the most famous Gaelic poet is Alasdair MacMhaighstir Alasdair (Alexander MacDonald) (*c.*1695–*c.*1770), a first cousin of Flora MacDonald. He was born at Dalelia, in Moidart, son of the (Episcopal) minister of Eilean Fhianain. He worked in Ardnamurchan for the SSPCK as a schoolmaster from 1729, and produced a Gaelic dictionary for the Society in 1741. In 1745 he abandoned teaching to fight with Clanranald, and converted to Catholicism. He was a fervent Jacobite, and much of his poetry is political. Some of his non-political poetry 'transgressed good taste', and put off patrons. In 1751 he visited Edinburgh, and had his poems printed while he was there. He returned to Arisaig in about 1752 and stayed there until his death. In 1751 he published a collection of poetry under the title *Ais-eridh na Sean Chánain* (Resurrection of the Ancient Scottish Tongue). This was the first non-religious work to be published in Gaelic. His most famous poem is *Birlinn Chlann Ragnahill* (The Birlinn of Clanranald), written in about 1750 (translated by Hugh MacDiarmid, 1935), describing a sea voyage from South Uist to Carrickfergus. He was buried at Kilmory, as the weather was too bad to cross to Eilean Fhianain, in Loch Shiel, and he is commemorated by a clock on the tower of Arisaig Catholic church.

Ailean Dall (Allan Macdougall) (*c.*1750–1828) was born in Glencoe. He was blind, and Macdonnell of Glengarry became his patron. His work was edited by the schoolmaster poet Ewan Maclachlan. One of his poems was a bitter attack on the Lowland shepherds whom he regarded as responsible for the depopulation of the Highlands.

Ann Grant (1755–1838), daughter of the barrack-master at Fort Augustus, married James Grant, chaplain there, in 1779. She lived at Laggan, on Loch Lochy, and published *Letters from the Mountains* in 1803.

Ewan MacLachlan (1775–1822), was a poet and translator, the foremost Celtic scholar of his day. Educated in Fort William, he worked as private tutor, then won a scholarship to Aberdeen University.

Mary Cameron MacKellar (1836–90), another poet, was born at Corriebeg, on the northern shore of Loch Eil, and is buried in Kilmallie churchyard. Her *Songs and Poems* were published in 1881.

Lochaber in Literature

As well as the local poets mentioned above, the 'romance' of the Highlands has inspired much poetry written by others. Robert Burns (1759–96), for example, wrote *Highland Mary*, and *My Heart's in the Highlands*. James Hogg (1770–1835) wrote Jacobite verse including the famous lines 'Charlie he's my darling, the young Chevalier'. William Wordsworth (1770–1850) toured Scotland in 1803, and wrote *To a Highland Girl*, *Rob Roy's Grave*, and *The Solitary Reaper*.

Some works are specific to Lochaber. A prolific contemporary of Wordsworth was Sir Walter Scott (1771–1832), who wrote the words of *Bonny Dundee*, as well as *The Lord of the Isles*, and *Rob Roy*. Thomas Campbell (1777–1844) wrote a long poem entitled *Pilgrim of Glencoe* in 1842.

John Keats (1795–1821) climbed Ben Nevis as part of a tour of the Highlands in 1819, and wrote a sonnet on the summit.

Read me a lesson, Muse, and speak it loud
   Upon the top of Nevis, blind in mist!
I look into the chasms, and a shroud
   Vaporous doth hide them,—just so much I wist
Mankind do know of hell; I look o'erhead,
   And there is sullen mist,—even so much
Mankind can tell of heaven; mist is spread
   Before the earth, beneath me,—even such,
Even so vague is man's sight of himself!
   Here are the craggy stones beneath my feet,—
Thus much I know that, a poor witless elf,
   I tread on them,—that all my eye doth meet
Is mist and crag, not only on this height,
But in the world of thought and mental might!

Alfred, Lord Tennyson (1809–92), stayed with friends at Ardtornish

House, Morvern. William Edmondstoune Aytoun (1813–65) wrote poems including *The Widow of Glencoe*, and *The Burial-march of Dundee*, which includes the lines

Like a tempest down the ridges
Swept the hurricane of steel,
Rose the slogan of MacDonald –
Flashed the broadsword of Locheill!

Novelists, too, have been inspired by the scenery, and the romance of the Jacobites.

William Black (1841–98), the novelist and keen yachtsman commemorated by a lighthouse on Mull, wrote a novel called *In Far Lochaber* (1888). Robert Louis Stevenson (1850–94) wrote *Kidnapped* (1886), set in 1751. The hero, David Balfour (a lowland Whig Presbyterian), encounters Allan Breck, a Highland Catholic Jacobite. After escaping from a ship onto Erray, off Mull, Balfour took a ferry from Torosay on Mull to Kinlochaline in Morvern, where he saw an emigrant ship just inside mouth of Loch Aline. 'The inn at Kinlochaline was the most beggarly vile place that ever pigs were styed in, full of smoke, vermin, and silent Highlanders'. He then walked across to Kingairloch, from where he got a ferry to Lettermore in Appin. There Balfour witnessed the murder of Campbell of Glenure, met Allan Breck Stewart again, and James of the Glen, and found himself on the run from the redcoated soldiers and out of Lochaber.

Neil Munro (1864–1930), wrote Highland romances. The Kingshouse, at the top of Glencoe (Plate 15), where the Campbell soldiers are said to have met before the massacre of Glencoe, is described in *John Splendid* (1898). *Doom Castle* (1901) is set in 1745. John Buchan (1875–1940) wrote several adventures with Scottish settings. In *Mr Standfast* (1919), Richard Hannay is followed from Glasgow on his way to Skye. To avoid his pursuers he left the Oban steamer at Lochaline, and walked to Mallaig.

There are many Jacobite novels, including a trilogy by D.K. Broster (1878–1950): *The Flight of the Heron* (1925), *The Gleam in the North* (1927), and *The Dark Mile* (1929).

Compton Mackenzie (1883–1972) wrote several humorous novels based around the characters of Donald MacDonald of Ben Nevis and Hugh Cameron of Kilwhillie, who both lived near the Great Glen. The main ones are *Monarch of the Glen* (1941), and *Hunting the Fairies* (1949). Those satirised include the more romantic of the travel writers, overenthusiastic visiting Americans seeking the romance of the Highlands, the hiking movement, and the west Highland historian and photographer M.E.M. Donaldson and the large vernacular-style thatched house she built at Sanna, in Ardnamurchan.

Children of the Dead End (1914), by Patrick McGill (1889–1963), 'gives a vivid account of navvy life during the construction of the Kinlochleven Aluminium Works'.

Many of those who travelled through the area from the eighteenth century onwards wrote down their impressions. Those quoted in the text area listed in the bibliography. Some not only observed scenery, but met characters or coincided with key events. The poet Robert Southey, for example, accompanied Thomas Telford on his tour of inspection of work on the Caledonian Canal in 1819.

Music

After the Reformation the church disapproved of the use of music. The traditional instruments of the Highlands, as well as the human voice, were bagpipes, fiddles and the clarsach (a small harp). Later the piano-accordion became popular. By the eighteenth century, Gaelic dance tunes were entering the musical mainstream, and were for the first time being written down. They were played on fiddles more commonly than bagpipes. Several old musical instruments can be seen in the West Highland Museum.

The eighteenth century also saw a revival in interest in folk songs. Writers such as James Watson, Allan Ramsay, David Herd and Robert Burns gathered traditional songs but also rearranged them, and wrote new ones in the same style. The most famous song about Lochaber is probably *Lochaber No More: or the soldier's farewell to his love*, written by Allan Ramsay (1686–1758), and representing the words of a young soldier leaving his girlfriend.

> Farewell to Lochaber, farewell to my Jean
> Where heartsome wi' her I ha'e mony day been
> For Lochaber no more, Lochaber no more,
> We'll maybe return to Lochaber no more.

> These tears that I shed they are all for my dear,
> And no' for the dangers attending or weir;
> Tho' borne on rough seas to a far bloody shore,
> Maybe to return to Lochaber no more.

> Though hurricanes rise, though rise ev'ry wind,
> No tempest can equal the storm in my mind;
> Tho loudest of thunders or louder waves roar,
> There's nothing like leavin' my love on the shore.

> To leave thee behind me, my heart is sair pain'd,
> But by ease that's inglorious no fame can be gain'd;
> And beauty and love's the reward of the brave,
> And I maun deserve it before I can crave.

> Then glory, my Jeanie, maun plead my excuse,
> Since honour commands me, how can I refuse?
> Without it I ne'er can have merit for thee;
> And losing thy favour, I'd better not be.

> I go then, my lass, to win honour and fame;
> and if I should chance to come gloriously hame,
> I'll bring a heart to thee, with love running o'er,
> and then I'll leave thee an' Lochaber no more.

According to Donald MacCulloch, 'the wailing Highland lament of *Lochaber no More* sounds so eerily on the pipes that it had to be forbidden during the Peninsular War, on account of its depressing effect on the spirits of the troops'.

Architecture

As we have seen, the land is poor, and the landowners in general were also relatively poor. Few could afford the most fashionable architects.

Scots architects whose work can be seen in Lochaber include James Gillespie Graham (1777–1855), who designed Achnacarry Castle (started 1802), the Roman Catholic chapel (now the parish church) at Arisaig (1810–11) (Fig. 32), and possibly the Glenfinnan Monument (1815) (Plate 14). William Burn (1789–1870) designed the churches at Kilchoan (1827–9) (Plate 18) and Arisaig (1849). David Bryce (1803–76), who specialised in the 'Scottish baronial' style, built Glengarry Castle (1866–9) and an extension to Roshven (1857–9). John Honeyman (1831–1914) designed the Ballachulish Hotel (1877). William Leiper (1839–1916), designed Kinlochmoidart House (1885). Sir Robert Rowand Anderson (1834–1921) designed Glencoe House (1896–7). A.G.S. Mitchell (1856–1930), built Glenborrodale Castle (1898–1902).

Peter Macgregor Chalmers (1859–1922), designer of many Scottish churches, was responsible probably for Kiel, Lochaline (1898) (Fig. 34) and certainly for St Kiaran's, Achnacarry (1911) (Fig. 31). Reginald Fairlie (1883–1952) designed Roman Catholic churches at Roybridge (St Margaret's, 1929) (Fig. 37), Fort William (Immaculate Conception, 1933–4) and Mallaig (St Patrick's, 1935). He also worked on the abbey at Fort Augustus. Ian Lindsay (1906–66) designed the very simple Roman Catholic church at Invergarry (St Finan's, 1938).

Duncan Cameron (d.1899), a local architect, designed the Highland Hotel, Fort William (1895), the West Highland Hotel, Mallaig (1898–1900), and Glenlochy Distillery Maltings, just outside Fort William (1898–1900). One of the most prolific local architects was Alexander Ross of Inverness (1834–1925). His works include St Finan's Episcopal Church, Kinlochmoidart 1857–60), Glengarry Parish Church (1864–5) (Fig. 33), the McIntosh Memorial Church, Onich (1875), St Andrews Episcopal Church, Fort William (1879–84), the former St Andrews Episcopal School (1880), St Mary's Episcopal Church, Glencoe (1880), Ardtornish House (1885–91) (Plate 21), and in partnership with David Mackintosh, Duncansburgh Parish Church, Fort William (1881).

The most prominent English architects commissioned to work in Lochaber were Philip Webb (1831–1915), who designed Arisaig House (1863–4), the steading of Borrodale Farm (1864), and the Astley Hall in Arisaig (1893) (Fig. 48) and Edward W. Pugin (1834–75), son of the more famous Augustus Pugin, who designed the Roman Catholic church at Glenfinnan (1873).

Painting

The discovery by travellers of the scenery of the Highlands, and its adoption by romantic writers is reflected in art as well. Horatio McCulloch (1805–67) was perhaps the greatest interpreter of Highland scenery. A friend of Landseer, he contributed to the popular Victorian image of the Highlands as wild and romantic, with spectacular and empty scenery. His paintings include Inverlochy Castle (1857, National Gallery of Scotland) and Glencoe (1864, Glasgow Art Galleries). William McTaggart (1835–1910), born in Kintyre, also painted the scenery of the Highlands, though mainly worked in southern Argyll. Sir David Young Cameron (1865–1945) was another painter who interpreted the Highlands for a wider audience. Some late Victorian pointers went overboard in their images of swirling mists, waterfalls, shaggy cattle and unusual lighting effects. It is these, however, such as Alfred de Branski, whose works now sell well as reproductions.

Some works had an influence on public opinion. At least two paintings have used the emotive title *Lochaber No More*. John Blake MacDonald's most famous painting (in the McManus Galleries, Dundee), shows Charles Edward Stuart leaving Scotland for ever in 1746. A picture by John Watson Nicol (1856–1926), painted in 1883, is entitled *The Emigrants* or *Lochaber No More*. Now in the Fleming Collection in London, it shows an elderly couple on the deck of a ship, looking back at their homeland, and has come to symbolise the individual tragedies of the Clearances.

Photography

George Washington Wilson (1823–93) took photographs of some of the same places, such as Glencoe, which had been popularised by landscape painters.

Mary E.M. Donaldson (1876–1958), was driven, and later walked around the Highlands, studying history and taking photographs. Her two books on her travels in this area, *Wanderings in the Western Highlands and Islands,* and *Further Wanderings – mainly in Argyll,* are well worth reading, and some of her photographs can be seen in the Mallaig Heritage Centre.

Robert Moyes Adam (1885–1967), gardener and botanical illustrator, travelled in Scotland photographing landscape and flora. His collection is in St Andrews University Library, and can be viewed online at http://specialcollections.st-and.ac.uk.

PART II

GAZETTEER

KEY SITES TO VISIT

Geology and landscape

Much of the landscape of Lochaber is spectacular, but some of the geological features are too large fully to appreciate from ground level. The Lighthouse Museum at **Ardnamurchan Point** (10.13) has displays including an aerial photograph of the traces of a huge extinct volcano in the area. The **Parallel Roads of Glen Roy** are well worth seeing. The road up the glen is single-track, narrow and winding, but the view from the car park (NN 297 852: OS 41) is worth the effort. The parish minister in 1795 described the 'parallel roads' as 'one of the most stupendous monuments of human industry'. It was only in the nineteenth century that geologists correctly identified them not as roads made by giants, but as the shorelines of lochs created when melting ice was held back by natural dams. Whether seen as the work of giants or geological accidents, they are impressive, and demonstrate how in Lochaber landscape and geology still dominate despite thousands of years of human activity.

For those who do not approach Lochaber this way, **Glencoe** is worth visiting. **Glen Nevis** is very attractive, and although crowded in summer, the lack of through traffic gives it a more peaceful atmosphere. Energetic visitors can climb Ben Nevis. The path starts at the visitor centre and car park at Achintee (NN 124 729: OS 41).

Prehistoric

Compared with most of Argyll, the prehistoric remains in Lochaber are not particularly impressive. The best standing stone close to the road is probably the one at **Onich** (1.9) (Plate 1). Another well worth visiting is that at **Camas nan Geall**, Ardnamurchan (1.12) (Fig. 23).

Castles

The best, and the most accessible, are **Inverlochy** (4.7) (Plate 9), just north of Fort William, and **Tioram** (4.11) (Plate 10), north-west of Acharacle. Also worth a visit are the remains of the fort at **Fort William** (7.1) (Plate 8).

Churches

For a range of churches, from the simple elegance of the Free Church to the grandeur of the later Episcopal and Roman Catholic churches, just take a look around **Fort William**.

For 'spirit of place', you should visit one of the medieval church sites, with wonderful views, and full of atmosphere, particularly if their graveyards have been in continuous use. The best ones are **Cill Choirille** in Glen Spean (3.2) (Plate 7), and the two in Morvern, **St Fintan,** Mungasdail (3.23) and **Cill Choluimchille,** Keil (3.3). Otherwise try **Arisaig** (3.20) or **Kilchoan** (3.16). Other atmospheric graveyards (without churches, or not necessarily medieval) include **Camas nan Geall**, Ardnamurchan (3.7), **Kilfinnan**, at the head of Loch Lochy (3.17) (Fig. 25), and **Strontian** (5.31) (Fig. 38). And for those who can manage to get to them, the **burial isles** (3.10, 3.11) (Plate 11) are very special places.

The best collection of **late medieval carved graveslabs** is at Kiel (3.3) above Lochaline, in Morvern, now housed in the Old Session House. The two largest stones lie flat on the floor, with others fixed upright around the walls. Several show West Highland galleys (Plate 6), and one unusual example depicts a castle with a galley drawn up in front of it. A couple of the stones have been reused, with eighteenth-century dates and initials carved into the earlier decoration. There is the lower part of a cross shaft, with a fine figure of a bishop (Plate 4). There is also a fine free-standing cross to the south of the present church, overlooking the Sound of Mull (Plate 3).

Otherwise, what you should see depends on your taste. If you like simple but elegant Georgian, then the best of the Parliamentary churches is the one at **Acharacle** (5.1) (Plate 16). If you favour high Victorian, then you should head for the Roman Catholic church at **Glenfinnan** (5.14). Or for those who like early twentieth-century work, look for the churches built by Reginald Fairlie, such as St Margaret's at **Roybridge** (5.29) (Fig. 37).

Country Houses

Most can only be glimpsed from the road, though **Ardtornish House** (6.3) (Plate 21) can be seen from Lochaline, and some might argue it looks better from a distance. The gardens are open to the public. **Inverailort House** (6.15), one of the most visible, is a good example of a plain Georgian house, added to by the Victorians. **Glencoe House** (6.13), even reduced in size, impresses by the sheer scale of what was really a holiday house. Some, such as **Glengarry Castle** (6.14), are perhaps more significant for their landscape setting than their architecture. **Glenborrodale Castle** (6.12) and **Kinlochmoidart House** (6.19) are among the more attractive of the late Victorian houses. Of the smaller houses, **Letterfinlay** (6.20) (Fig. 41) is plain and solid, being built as barracks or an inn. **Ballachulish House** (6.5) is also plain, though much larger, while **Dalelia** (6.8) (Plate 23) is charming.

Rural Settlement

There are many deserted settlements to choose from, but perhaps the most atmospheric site is **Camas nan Geall** (NM 559 618: OS 47) (Plate 19), in Ardnamurchan, with its evidence of settlement from the Bronze Age to the nineteenth century, situated in a south-facing bay, with further remains on the surrounding hills. **Inniemore**, in Morvern (NM 655 518: OS 49), has paths and interpretation boards provided by the Forestry Commission. But almost anywhere you explore you may come across evidence of areas which were once inhabited and farmed but are now abandoned.

Industry and Transport

For sheer size and ingenuity, the **Caledonian Canal** cannot fail to impress, and in particular Neptune's Staircase (Fig. 50). Elsewhere it is notable for being the only level feature in an undulating landscape. Also impressive however often you see it is the **Glenfinnan Railway Viaduct** (10.35) (Plate 27). The anachronistically named 'Jacobite Steam Train' runs along this line during the summer.

For the more adventurous, traces of the **lead mines** above Strontian can still be seen, but the best involve some walking. The **slate quarries** of Ballachulish can be seen from the road. East Laroch (NN 08 58: OS 41) is now laid out with walks and information boards, and you can climb the path on the west side for a fine view from the top.

Monuments

The **Glenfinnan Monument** (12.5) (Plate 14) and the **Commando Monument** (12.8) (Plate 29) are the most impressive, both in their own right and within their landscape settings.

West Highland Museum

The West Highland Museum was established in 1922, though it did not acquire a permanent home in Fort William until 1926. The collections are wide-ranging, and include the best assemblage of Jacobite relics in the world. Whatever your interests, there is something here for you. It really is well worth a visit.

1. PREHISTORIC SITES –
RITUAL AND FUNERARY

Lochaber is not rich in prehistoric monuments. The most prolific ritual and funerary sites in this area are cairns. Some are chambered, and some have a kerb – a ring of upright stones marking the outer edge. Occasionally the kerb stones are all that survives, and these were sometimes misinterpreted by nineteenth-century antiquarians as stone circles. Many of the surviving cairns are marked on OS maps, but they may be overgrown, particularly in the summer.

1.1   Acharn to Kinlochaline, Morvern

Eleven cairns along the valley of the river Aline

Acharn Bridge   NM 702 504: OS 49

A kerb cairn

Acharn   NM 697 507: OS 49

A cairn

Acharn   NM 697 505: OS 49

Three cairns

Claggan   NM 697 493: OS 49

Three kerb cairns, excavated in 1973–74 (Plate 2). Material from them produced radiocarbon dates of between 1058 and 462 BC.

Kinlochaline NM692 474; 695 476: OS 49

Three cairns

1.2   Achnaha, Morvern NM 648 453: OS 49

A kerb cairn

1.3   Ballachulish Home Farm NN 048 596: OS 41

A cairn with five kerb stones remaining. There was originally a cist at the centre.

1.4   Beinn Bhan NM 659 492: OS 49

A standing stone west-north-west of the summit

1.5   Carn an Rubha, Ballachulish NN 054 599: OS 41

The southern half of a cairn, the rest having been robbed. A few kerb stones survive, and it is said to have contained cist burials.

1.6   Carnliath, south-east of Rahoy, Morvern
  NM 644 559: OS 49

A chambered cairn

1.7   Carn na Cailliche, Rhemore, Morvern
  NM 578 503: OS 49

A cairn

1.8   Carnoch, Glen Tarbert NM 847 608: OS 40

A kerb cairn, with many granite kerb stones still in situ

1.9   Clach-a-Charra, Onich (Plate 1) NN 026 613: OS 41

A seven-foot tall, water-worn stone, pierced by two holes, thought to be natural. This stone was traditionally associated with the revenge killing of the two sons of Cummin of Inverlochy by a wronged clansman.

1.10 Clach Aindreis, Swordle, Ardnamurchan
NM 547 707: OS 47

A chambered cairn

1.11 Cladh Chatian (St Cathan's Stone), Kilmory, Ardnamurchan
NM 526 695: OS 47

A standing stone

1.12 Cladh Chiarain, Camas nan Geall, Ardnamurchan
NM 560 619: OS 47

A chambered cairn, partly destroyed by the construction of adjacent buildings

A Bronze Age standing stone with added Christian carvings
(Fig. 23)
NM 560 618: OS 47

1.13 Dun Dige, Glen Nevis
NN 125 719: OS 40

A cairn, sometimes described as a motte

1.14 Duror, south of Duror church
NM 987 545: OS 49

A standing stone, an impressive 3.7 m high

1.15 Glen Etive
NN 143 476: OS 50

A well-preserved cairn, beside the River Etive, south of Invercharnan

A cairn at the head of Loch Etive
NN 112 455: OS 50

Fig. 23. Bronze Age standing stone, later decorated with Christian motifs, Camas nan Geall (after RCAHMS) (1.12 and 3.7)

1.16　Greadal Fhinn, Ardnamurchan　　　NM 476 639: OS 47

A chambered cairn

1.17　Inverailort　　　　　　　　　　　NM 763 815: OS 40

A cairn

1.18　Kilchoan, Ardnamurchan　　NM 487 631; 497 632: OS 47

Well-preserved cairns on the coast to the west of the pier

1.19　Killundine, Morvern　　　　　　NM 586 496: OS 47

Two kerb cairns, partly robbed

1.20　Loch Eilt　　　　　　　　　　　NM 801 828: OS 40

A cairn

1.21 North Ballachulish   NN 054 601: OS 41

A ritual site, between the road towards Kinlochleven and the loch. The 4 ft 6 in high female figure known as the 'Ballachulish Venus', now in the Museum of Scotland, was found here in 1880 (Fig. 2). She was discovered surrounded by interwoven branches and twigs, suggesting that she may have been housed within a wattled hut or shrine. Originally thought to be Viking or Celtic, the figure has been radiocarbon-dated to between 600 and 500 BC.

1.22 North Ballachulish   NN 057 599: OS 41

On a promontory sticking out into Loch Leven are a number of cup-marks on the top of a rock, some probably genuinely Bronze Age, others possibly natural features

1.23 Rahoy, Morvern   NM 644 559: OS 49

The remains of a chambered cairn, on the northern shore of Loch Teacuis

1.24 Resipole, Sunart   NM 716 647: OS 40

A kerb cairn

1.25 Rubha Dearg, Morvern
NM 664 444; 662 444; 661 444: OS 49

Three cairns, west of Lochaline

1.26 Rubha Mhor, North Ballachulish   NN 051 601: OS 41

A cairn

1.27 Salen, Ardnamurchan   NM 689 649, 686 652: OS 40

Cairns

2. PREHISTORIC SITES –
DOMESTIC AND DEFENSIVE

Those listed below are the few which are visible today. Forts and duns can be found marked on OS maps, but many have been heavily robbed, and most will be heavily overgrown during the summer.

2.1 Allt Sordail, Ardnamurchan NM 553 693: OS 47

South-south-east of Swordle, a heavily robbed dun

2.2 An Dun, west of Kinlochmoidart NM 682 735: OS 40

A dun

2.3 Caisteal Breac (Dun Borodil), Glenborrodale
NM 612 615: OS 40

A dun

2.4 Caisteal nan Con, Morvern NM 583 486: OS 47

The promontory was protected by two walls, both severely robbed. One stretch of the inner wall has been used as part of the outbuildings of the later castle.

2.5 Camas nan Geall, Ardnamurchan NM 554 615: OS 47

On a small promontory to the west of the bay are the remains of a stone-walled fort, Sgeir Fhada, much of which has collapsed off the edge of the cliff

2.6 Cnocan Dubh, Ballachulish   NN 080 585: OS 41

North of East Laroch, a stone-walled fort on a rocky outcrop, its inner and outer walls now tumbled and covered by grass

2.7 Dun an Eididh, E side of Kentra bay   NM 646 692: OS 40

West-north-west of Duneira, a dun

2.8 Dun Ban, Sanna, Ardnamurchan   NM 448 704: OS 47

Remains of a promontory fort

2.9 Dun Deardail, Glen Nevis   NN 127 701: OS 41

A vitrified fort, pear-shaped in plan, whose walls at the end of the eighteenth century still stood between 2 and 4 feet high

2.10 Dun Fhionnairadh, Fiunary, Morvern
NM 614 469: OS 49

A prominent site seen above the road when travelling east, but the oval wall which once enclosed the summit has been quarried for farm buildings

2.11 Dun Ghallain, Ardnamurchan   NM 647 600: OS 40

West of Salen, a dun, 11 by 13 m internally, with an outwork of boulders

2.12 Dun Resipol, close to the road   NM 719 639: OS 40

A heavily-robbed fort

2.13 Eilean Loch Airceig   NN 159 888: OS 41

A crannog (and medieval chapel)

2.14 Eilean nan Gobhar, Loch Ailort (opposite Roshven)
NM 693 793; 693 794: OS 40

Two vitrified forts

2.15 Eilean Tigh Na Slige, Loch Treig   NN 347 768: OS 41

A crannog excavated when the loch level was temporarily lowered during the construction in 1933 of the Lochaber Water Power Scheme. It was found to have been in use in the first century AD, and reused in the seventeenth century. Finds from it, including a possible logboat, and a probable bog-butter trough, are in the West Highland Museum.

2.16 Eilean Uillne, NNW of Mains of Drimnin, Morvern
NM 545 565: OS 47

A fort

2.17 Lag nam Morag, Ballachulish   NN 030 619: OS 41

A fort, about 23 by 15 m. The wall is tumbled and covered with turf.

2.18 Loch nan Eala, Arisaig   NM 667 857: OS 40

A crannog, excavated in 1856

2.19 Loch Oich, near Invergarry   NH 318 007; 327 018: OS 34

Two crannogs

2.20 Loch Tearnait, Morvern   NM 748 470: OS 49

A crannog, in about 12 feet of water, with no trace of a causeway. It may well have been used in the medieval period, being on the route between the castles of Glensanda and Kinlochaline. The name 'Tearnait' signifies 'refuge'.

2.21 Mingary Pier — NM 492 628: OS 47

A fort, almost robbed away

2.22 Port Mor, 'Mungasdail Castle', Morvern — NM 560 530: OS 47

The remains of a dun

2.23 Rahoy, Morvern — NM 633 564: OS 49

A dun with thick vitrified walls, and the floor inside artificially levelled

2.24 Risga, Ardnamurchan — NM 610 600: OS 49

The only excavated Mesolithic site in the area. At this, and at other casual find sites, there is little or nothing to see today. It is possible, however, that while walking one may come across a pile of discarded shells, or the waste from the manufacture of flint tools, which may date from this period.

2.25 Rubh Aird Ghamhsgail, Arisaig — NM 692 840: OS 40

A good example of a vitrified fort

2.26 Rubha na h-Uamha, Ardnamurchan — NM 565 712: OS 47

On a remote headland, a very well-preserved dun, with walls between 1.2 and 4.3 m (4 to 14 ft) thick, and standing up to 2.4 m (nearly 8 ft) high. There are two entrances, one at each end.

2.27 The Torr, Shielfoot — NM 662 701: OS 40

A univallate fort, mostly vitrified, on a knife-edge ridge, with an outer wall on the south side. At the north-east end a probable dun seems to overlie the fort.

2.28 Torr an Duin, Loch nan Gabhar, Ardgour

NM 970 633: OS 40

A fort excavated in 1908. Traces of vitrification were found.

West Highland Museum

Among the objects in the collections are neolithic flints from Sanna and Gorton, both on Ardnamurchan; a possible logboat from Loch Treig; and Bronze Age finds including a pair of gold armlets from Kilmallie, and an axe found near Spean Bridge.

3. EARLY CHRISTIAN AND MEDIEVAL RELIGIOUS SITES

3.1 Ardslignish, Ardnamurchan   NM 563 610: OS 47

A burial ground within a D-shaped enclosure

3.2 Cill Choirille (St Cyril), near Roybridge (Plate 7)
NN 306 812: OS 41

A fifteenth-century church, said to be one of seven built by Locheil as a penance. The others are Cill Donnain (Glengarry), Kilmallie, Kilchoan, Arisaig, Morvern and Laggan (Loch Lochy) (or Eilean Munde, in Loch Leven). It stood roofless for many years until it was restored in 1932–33 as a Roman Catholic church, paid for by the descendants of emigrants to Nova Scotia. Near the door is a monument to Iain Lom MacDonald, the bard of Keppoch. The burial ground is still in use, and the site is spectacular and atmospheric.

3.3 Cill Choluimchille (St Columba), Kiel, Morvern
NM 671 451: OS 49

Fragmentary, though high quality and attractive elements of the medieval church survive in the churchyard (Plate 5). To the south of the church, overlooking the Sound of Mull, is a free-standing cross (Plate 3) (Fig. 5). In the Old Session House, to the east of the church, is a fine collection of carved grave slabs, mostly of the fifteenth century (Plates 4, 6).

3.4 Cill Donnain, Glengarry   NH 265 027: OS 34

The burial ground, now disused, is circular, and may therefore be early. A raised area in the south-east corner may be the site of an early church, dedicated to St Donan.

3.5   Cill Mhairi, Kilmory, Ardnamurchan NM 532 699: OS 47

There is no trace of the medieval chapel which once stood here, but the burial ground survives, and a fragment of a free-standing ringed cross.

3.6   Cille Mhaodain, Ardgour   NN 012 656: OS 41

This small burial ground marks the site of an early church, and attached is the burial ground of the Macleans of Ardgour.

3.7   Cladh Chiarain, Camus nan Geall, Ardnamurchan
NM 560 618: OS 47

A very atmospheric site, only approachable on foot, consisting of several abandoned settlements. At the heart of the fertile ground at the head of the bay is a small burial ground, containing some interesting eighteenth-century carved headstones, including one with a crucifixion in bold relief, and one with heraldic decoration. Both are in the Irish rather than the Scottish tradition. There is also a prehistoric standing stone to which Christian carving has been added (Fig. 23).

3.8   Cranachan, Glen Roy   NN 295 846: OS 41

A cross-incised stone, said to have been used as an altar by Roman Catholic priests in the seventeenth and early eighteenth centuries when Roman Catholics were persecuted.

3.9   Crois Bheinn, Morvern   NM 594 542: OS 47

A cross-marked 'roughly-fashioned and battered cruciform stone', at the highest point of the old track between Drimnin and Loch Teacuis.

3.10   Eilean Fhianain, St Finan's Isle or the Green Isle, Loch Shiel   NM 752 683: OS 40

St Finan is said to have come here and lived in a cell on the island. After his death in 575 it became a place of pilgrimage. On the island are the ruins of a late sixteenth-century chapel, 70 ft long, built by Allan, chief of Clanranald. On the altar is (or was) a small Celtic bronze bell. There are also stone crosses. Around it is the burial ground of the MacDonalds of Clanranald, and more generally for the population of Moidart, Sunart and Ardnamurchan. It lies at the centre of a network of coffin roads, complete with resting cairns.

3.11   Eilean Munde, Loch Leven (Plate 11)   NN 083 591: OS 41

Burial place of the Camerons of Callart, the MacDonalds of Glencoe (including those killed in the massacre of 1692) and the Stewarts of Ballachulish. At the west end of the island is the ruined chapel, probably late medieval and originally the parish church of St Mun. The floor has been raised by burials, as has the surrounding ground. In the mid seventeenth century the part of the parish on the northern side of the loch was absorbed into Kilmallie (Inverness-shire) while that on the southern shore was absorbed into Appin and Lismore (Argyll), whose parish church was at Duror. The last service was held here in 1653, but burials continued into the twentieth century. Various funerary monuments survive, three medieval, and several post-Reformation (Fig. 24), including one with a quaint relief carving showing Duncan Mackenzie, tenant at North Ballachulish, in Highland dress, killing a dragoon at the battle of Prestonpans in 1745 (Plate 12). The stone was erected in the early nineteenth century by his grandson. Also on the island is the burial enclosure of the MacDonalds of Glencoe. Macculloch described the island as 'crowded with gravestones and ornaments, and with sculptures which, in a place so remote and unexpected, attract an attention that more splendid works would scarcely command in the midst of civilization'.

Fig. 24. Gravestone, Eilean Munde, Glencoe (3.11)

3.12 Glenfinnan   NM 906 806: OS 40

The old burial ground of Dail Naoimh, near the monument

3.13 Glengarry, Greenfield   NN 202 005: OS 34

A circular burial ground

3.14 Isle of Reeds, Inverailort   NM 773 824: OS 40

A burial isle in the river Ailort

3.15 Keil, Duror   NM 971 538: OS 49

A chapel, probably late medieval, dedicated to St Columba. Burials within the walls have raised the floor level, and the walls have been much repaired. There are no visible pre-1707 monuments.

3.16   Kilchoan, Ardnamurchan   NM 485 640: OS 47

The ruins of the old parish church (mainly eighteenth-century, but both gable ends probably survive from the twelfth- or thirteenth-century church). In the graveyard, though neglected and obscured by long grass, are two Iona-style graveslabs of the fourteenth or fifteenth century, decorated with floriated crosses and hunting scenes.

3.17   Kilfinnan, Loch Lochy (Fig. 25)   NN 278 957: OS 34

A graveyard which dates back to at least 1699, and is still in use. The unusually tall burial enclosure may be part of the remains of St Finan's church. The dedication, and position, suggest that this was an early church site.

3.18   Killundine, Morvern   NM 579 498: OS 47

Near a nineteenth-century family burial ground can be seen the remains of a rectangular building set within a small D-shaped enclosure. While the remains may be medieval, the position, the finding here of two early-Christian cross-marked stones, and the dedication to St Fintan, suggest that this is an early Christian site, probably the earliest in Morvern. It has been suggested that this was the site of the monastery established by St Fintan, a follower of Columba.

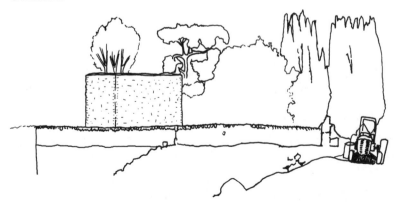

Fig. 25. The isolated graveyard at Kilfinnan, Loch Lochy (3.17)

3.19   Kilmallie, Corpach   NN 090 769: OS 41

The remains of an older church, possibly seventeenth-century, have been re-used as a burial enclosure for the Camerons of Locheil. The site is of great antiquity, with a very early Christian church being sited somewhere in this area (as indicated by the place name Annat), and dedicated to Maillidh. Local tradition claims that its successor was one of seven churches built by Locheil as a penance.

3.20   Kilmory, Arisaig   NM 658 869: OS 40

The ruins of St Maelruba's Church, built in 1574, with wall monuments and relocated graveslabs with hunting scenes. It is surrounded by an oval burial ground, probably later in date, and still in use. The earliest church is said to have been down on the shore, on the site of Keppoch house.

3.21   Loch Arkaig, St Columba's Chapel   NN 159 888: OS 41

On the highest point of an island near the foot of Loch Arkaig stand the remains of an old chapel dedicated to St Columba, of unknown date but in use in the seventeenth century. Around it was a graveyard, once the burial place of the MacPhees, and later used by the Camerons of Locheil after they moved to Achnacarry.

3.22   Meall Doire, Glen Spean   NN 290 812: OS 41

A cross-incised stone

3.23   St Fintan, Mungasdail, Morvern   NM 564 538: OS 47

The old parish church of the parish of Killintag, within its graveyard. The church was in use until 1780, but is now ruined, a grassy mound with burials inside it. A modern extension of the burial ground is still in use, despite the lack of vehicular access. A very atmospheric site, with fine views to Mull and Ardnamurchan.

4. CASTLES AND FORTIFIED HOUSES

4.1 Ardtornish Castle, Morvern (Figs 4 and 26)
NM 691 426: OS 49

Built probably in the late thirteenth century. Ardtornish, like Aros on Mull, was a hall house. Later a stronghold of the Lords of the Isles, it stands on a prominent site, overlooking the eastern half of the Sound of Mull, and intervisible with Duart and Aros. To the north and east are traces of a number of small buildings, which are probably contemporary with the castle. In 1462 John, fourth Lord of the Isles, signed the Treaty of Ardtornish and Westminster, an

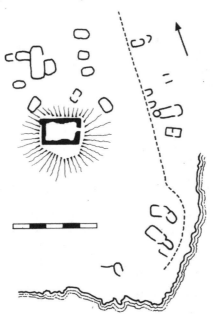

Fig. 26. Plan of Ardtornish Castle, with traces of small buildings of unknown date adjacent to it (after RCAHMS) (4.1)

alliance with the English king, Edward IV, against the King of Scotland. After the forfeiture of the Lordship of the Isles in 1493 the lands of Ardtornish seem to have become the property of the Macleans of Duart, and then by the end of the seventeenth century of the Campbell earls of Argyll. Sir Walter Scott described Ardtornish as standing 'on its frowning steep, twixt cloud and ocean hung'. But, being a hall house, the ruins were much less impressive than those of taller castles, and in 1910–15 the ruins were 'restored', and the silhouette of the building 'improved', though on the evidence of early photographs not too drastically.

4.2 Caisteal Dubh nan Cliar (Ormisbaig), Ardnamurchan
NM 473 631: OS 47

A very small ruin on the coast west of Kilchoan, dating possibly to the sixteenth or seventeenth century, and possibly related to nearby Mingary Castle

4.3 Caisteal nan Con, Morvern NM 583 486: OS 47

The attractive ruin of a late seventeenth-century house, built in a form transitional between the tower house and later more horizontal houses, and consisting of a three-storey rectangular block with a projecting stair tower. Despite its name, 'castle of the dogs', which suggests it may have been a hunting lodge, it seems to have been the main residence of the Macleans of Killundine. It seems to have had a short life, being abandoned by the mid-eighteenth century in favour of a mansion up on the hill (now demolished). It stands within a prehistoric fort, with a sheltered bay on its landward side providing a safe landing place for boats.

4.4 Drimnin Castle, Morvern NM 548 549: OS 47

Probably dating from the late sixteenth century or later, and abandoned in the mid eighteenth century, replaced by a laird's house slightly inland (6.9). The remains of the castle were demolished in 1838, when a Roman Catholic chapel was built on the site by the owner, Charles Gordon. Traces of one wall remain to the west of the west end of the church, which is itself now roofless.

4.5   Glensanda, Morvern   NM 823 468: OS 49

An oblong tower house, on a rocky site overlooking the mouth of the Glensanda river, probably built in the late fifteenth century by Maclean of Kingairloch. It is constructed of local pink granite, and has two storeys and an attic. It stands on the top of a 150 foot high rock, and opposite Castle Coeffin on Lismore.

4.6   Invergarry Castle, Great Glen (Fig. 27)
NH 315 006: OS 34

Probably dating from the early seventeenth century, a Z-plan tower house on the north-west shore of Loch Oich, now in the grounds of the Glengarry Castle Hotel (but fenced to prevent access, because it is unstable). Invergarry was the seat of the Macdonnells (or MacDonalds) of Glengarry. Burnt by General Monk in 1654, it had been repaired by 1691, and was used by a government garrison between 1692 and 1715, but was burnt down in 1716. It was at least partially restored as accommodation for the managers of a local iron furnace in the 1720s. Glengarry returned briefly in 1731, and the Prince stayed here both before and after Culloden. The castle was blown up by the Duke of Cumberland's army soon afterwards, and was subsequently abandoned.

4.7   Inverlochy Castle (Plate 9; Fig. 3)   NN 120 754: OS 41

Built by the Comyns of Lochaber in the late thirteenth century as the seat of the Lordship of Lochaber, but lost soon afterwards in 1307 to Robert the Bruce during the Wars of Independence. It stands at the mouth of the river Lochy, which once also filled a ditch surrounding

Fig. 27. Invergarry Castle from the north-east (from MacGibbon & Ross, Castellated and Domestic Architecture*)*

the other three sides. Although low-lying, the castle guarded the south-west entrance to the Great Glen, and the junction of Loch Linnhe and Loch Eil. Its design is fairly simple, roughly square, with a tower at each corner, and entrances in the north and south walls. The north-west tower was larger than the rest, and served as the keep. Restored by the earl of Huntly in 1509, it became the seat of the sheriff of Lochaber. The battlements on the west wall were added in *c.*1905.

4.8   Kinlochaline, Morvern (Fig. 11)   NM 697 476: OS 49

A tower house standing on a rocky ridge overlooking the mouth of the river Aline at the head of Loch Aline, it was probably built by the Macleans of Duart in the fifteenth century. Remodelled in about 1600, it was held by royalist troops in 1644. In 1679 it was attacked by the ninth earl of Argyll. Maclean of Kingairloch got it back, only for

Fig. 28. Mingary Castle from the north-west (from MacGibbon & Ross, Castellated and Domestic Architecture)

it to be surrendered to the tenth earl of Argyll in 1690. The building was repaired in about 1890 by Valentine Smith of Ardtornish, and has recently been completely restored and is now inhabited again.

4.9   Leanachan, Glen Spean   NN 218 784: OS 41

An early medieval motte or castle site

4.10   Mingary Castle, Ardnamurchan (Fig. 28)
NM 502 631: OS 47

Just to the east of Kilchoan, in an impressive location, guarding the northern end of the Sound of Mull and the entrance to Loch Sunart. It is polygonal in shape, built to fit the rock on which it stands, with a rock-cut ditch on the landward side. The walls are thickest and highest on the landward sides, and crenellated. What survives is a simple curtain wall, with little trace of the original interior buildings. Built in the thirteenth century for the Lords of the Isles, it was besieged in 1515 and 1517, when it was taken and partly destroyed. The castle was remodelled in the late sixteenth century, with improved defences, and in 1588 was held by MacIan of Ardnamurchan and besieged by Maclean of Duart (with the help of some Spanish soldiers borrowed from the Spanish Armada ship anchored off Tobermory). The bay in front of the castle is called Port nan Spaindeach. The castle was besieged again in 1644, when it was captured by Alastair McColla, but retaken in 1647 by the Parliamentarian General Leslie. It subsequently became the property of the Campbells. The present interior building, a three storey and attic block, dates from around 1720, but probably stands on the site of the original hall.

4.11   Castle Tioram, Moidart (Plate 10; Fig. 29)
NM 662 724: OS 40

Described by the local minister in 1838 as 'a memorial to the times when the shout of armed clans and the clang of the conflict disturbed the silence of these still waters, and now peaceful solitudes'. It stands at the head of Loch Moidart, on a rocky island accessible at low tide. Built for Lady Anne MacRuari, the divorced wife of John, first Lord of Isles, in around the middle of the fourteenth century, it passed to the MacDonalds of Clanranald in 1493. Originally of a similar plan to Mingary, its polygonal walls enclosed a rectangular keep, perhaps dating from the fourteenth century, and a south range of buildings, possibly also fourteenth century, which had another two floors added in around 1600, creating a tower which stands up above the curtain wall, with corbelled round turrets on three corners.

4.12   Tor Castle, Great Glen   NN 132 785: OS 41

'Of old, when firearms were unknown, it certainly was a very strong place' (*Old Statistical Account*), as 'it stands on the brink of a frightful precipice'. The first castle on this site was said to have been the home of Banquo in the tenth century. The second, built in the eleventh century, was the home of the Mackintoshes until 1291, and was seized by the Camerons in about 1380. It had been rebuilt by the

Fig. 29. Castle Tioram from the south-west (from MacGibbon & Ross, Castellated and Domestic Architecture*)*

sixteenth century, but in the late seventeenth century the Camerons moved to Achnacarry. The castle was abandoned after 1745, and very little remains. 'Banquo's Walk', a quarter of a mile north of the castle (NN 133 791 to 136 795), is probably part of the sixteenth- or seventeenth-century approach road, the nearer part of which was lost under the grounds of the later house.

5. POST-REFORMATION CHURCHES AND GRAVEYARDS

5.1 Acharacle, Ardnamurchan (Plate 16)   NM 675 683: OS 40

A Parliamentary church, designed and built by William Thomson in 1829–33, but a variant on the standard design, having large windows in both long sides. Rectangular, not T-plan, its interior was altered *c.*1930, but it still has the original diamond-pane windows. It is unusual in having a carriage drive leading past the front.

NM 676 682: OS 40

The castellated gateway leading from the road into the lower graveyard was erected *c.*1920 as a war memorial (Fig. 30). The Parliamentary manse also survives. Built in 1829–33, it conforms to Telford's plan,

Fig. 30. The war memorial gate at Acharacle Church (5.1)

Fig. 31. St Kiaran's Church, Achnacarry (5.2)

being single-storey and H-shaped, with two rooms and an entrance hall in the central block, and two more in each wing (Fig. 7).

5.2   Achnacarry, St Kiaran's Church (Fig. 31)

NN 181 873: OS 41

Designed by P. MacGregor Chalmers in the early Christian style. Built in 1911, it stands deep in the woods, on an unsurfaced estate road, situated between the big house and the village, with a carriage drive up to the door.

5.3   Ardgour   NN 010 641: OS 40

A Parliamentary church, built in 1829 to the design of William Thomson. The building has undergone various alterations, including blocking the original doors, and adding a crenellated porch at the east end, but still retains some of its character.

Fig. 32. Former Roman Catholic Church, now parish church, Arisaig (5.4)

5.4   Arisaig, Parish Church (Fig. 32)   NM 661 864: OS 40

Built as a Roman Catholic chapel in 1810–11, to a simple design by James Gillespie Graham. Its small size is emphasised by the pair of quite large two-storey houses either side of it. These were the manse and the schoolhouse, though when Lord Teignmouth visited in 1836 he was puzzled to find a Protestant missionary living in the manse, though the church was Roman Catholic.

5.5   Arisaig, St Mary's Roman Catholic Church
NN 658 869: OS 40

Designed by William Burn and built in 1849. The clock in the tower was added in 1928 in memory of Alastair MacMhaigstir Alastair, the Gaelic poet, who was buried here. There is also a 'fine Presbytery House'.

5.6   Ballachulish, St John's Episcopal Church
NN 066 584: OS 41

Built in 1842–8, with a chancel added in 1888, it stands beside the main A82. Its graveyard contains a fine collection of nineteenth-century slate headstones.

5.7   Corpach, Kilmallie Parish Church   NN 090 769: OS 41

Built in 1781–3, with a birdcage bellcote with crown spire on top. It was altered in 1889–90, including new windows, when D.Y. Cameron designed the minister's chair and elders' stalls. It has some colourful late twentieth-century stained glass. The church stands within a circular enclosure, next to an older one, also circular, within which is the burial place of Camerons of Fassfern, whose walls may incorporate the remains of the early sixteenth-century church.

5.8   Craigs Burial Ground, Fort William   NN 107 742: OS 41

Originally the burial ground for the eighteenth-century fort. Its entrance arch, erected here in 1896, was originally the main entrance to the 1690 fort (Plate 8).

5.9   Drimnin, St Columba's Roman Catholic Chapel
NM 548 550: OS49

Designed by James Anderson and built in 1838 on the site of Drimnin Castle. Now roofless, it is an example of the effort and expense some landowners would go to to provide themselves and their families with an appropriate place of worship.

5.10   Duror, Appin   NM 993 552: OS 49

A T-plan Parliamentary church, built in 1827, of rubble with dressings of pink sandstone. There is a birdcage belfry in the south-west gable, and the original windows with cast-iron mullions and small panes survive on the north-west side. Behind it a manse of the same date (NM 994 552) (now a private house, and with bay windows added).

5.11 Duror, Appin, St Adamnan's Episcopal Church
NM 994 555: OS 49

A charming little church, built in 1848, with a porch added in 1871, and a chancel in 1911. The north window, and possibly also the east window, are by Ninian Comper, 1919.

5.12 Fernish, Morvern
NM 566 522: OS 49

Morvern was once two parishes, and until recently retained two churches, and both burial grounds are still in use. In 1780 the medieval church of St Fintan, near Mungasdail, was replaced by a new building further east, on the old road. Its successor, above the present road (563 523), was built in 1892, paid for by Mrs Cheape of Killundine.

5.13 Gairlochy
NN 176 841: OS 41

The burial place of MacMartins of Letterfinlay, in use from the eighteenth century or earlier, and still in use. Some graves were originally marked by iron 'pigs' from the eighteenth-century furnace at Glengarry.

5.14 Glenfinnan, Our Lady and St Finnan Roman Catholic Church
NM 903 808: OS 40

A large Gothic structure designed by E.W. Pugin and built in 1873, the only work by him in the Highlands, and a very impressive building. Its large bronze bell hangs in a wooden frame nearby, reputedly because it proved to large and heavy to lift into the belfry.

5.15 Glen Nevis, Tom Eas an t-Slinnean
NN 120 727: OS 41

The burial ground of the MacSorlies of Glen Nevis, a branch of Clan

Cameron. Dating from the eighteenth century or earlier, it is still in occasional use. Those commemorated include some who worked in Fort William/Gordonsburgh, including a clog-maker. A mortsafe cage from here is now in the West Highland Museum. Its woodland setting gives it a distinctive atmosphere.

5.16   Glenuig, St Agnes Roman Catholic Church
NM 670 773: OS 40

Built *c.*1850. Very plain and solid.

5.17   Invergarry, Glengarry Parish Church (Fig. 33)
NH 304 010: OS 34

Designed by Alexander Ross, and built in 1864–5, with additions, including the tower, in 1896–7

5.18   Invergarry, St Finan's Roman Catholic Church
NH 309 007: OS 34

Designed by Ian Lindsay in 1938, in conjunction with Peter F. Anson, a prominent Catholic historian. The result is regarded by some as a rather artificial simplicity.

Fig. 33. Glengarry Parish Church, Invergarry (5.17)

Fig. 34. Kiel Church, Cross and Session House, Morvern (5.20)

5.19   Inverlochy   NN 120 752: OS 41

A burial ground, still in use, but said originally to have been reserved for the descendants of those who fought in the Battle of Inverlochy in 1645

5.20   Kiel, Lochaline (Fig. 34)   NM 670 451: OS 49

Parish church of St Columba, built 1898, a plain design by P. MacGregor Chalmers, replacing an earlier building on the same site

5.21   Kilchoan, the former Ardnamurchan Parish Church
NM 485 640: OS 47

Dedicated to St Congan, built in 1762–3 at the expense of the owner of Ardnamurchan, incorporating some of the fabric of the medieval church, but now standing roofless. In front of the graveyard is the manse (NM 484 638), built *c.*1790, with a front block and outbuildings added in 1828-30.

5.22   Kilchoan, Ardnamurchan Parish Church (Plate 18)
NM 488 638: OS 47

'Durable and well-constructed', designed by William Burn in

Fig. 35. The mission church at Kingairloch, parish of Ardgour (5.23)

the Tudor style, built 1827–31, and paid for by the laird, Sir James Riddell

5.23 Kingairloch, a mission church (Fig. 35)
NM 861 525: OS 49

Built in 1857, with an apse and some good stained glass windows added in 1906. An attractive building serving a small, isolated community.

5.24 Kinlochmoidart, St Finan's Episcopal Church
NM 710 727: OS 40

Designed by Alexander Ross, built in 1857–60. It contains what may be some of the earliest stained glass windows in the Highlands, designed by Jemima Blackburn of Roshven (6.22), and dating somewhere between 1859 and 1873.

5.25 Mingarry, Roman Catholic Church   NM 686 695: OS 40

Large and solid

Fig. 36. A replica medieval cross outside St Bride's Episcopal Church, North Ballachulish (5.26)

5.26 North Ballachulish, St Bride's Episcopal Church
NN 052 610: OS 41

Built in 1875 by Lady Ewing. Near the door is a replica of a medieval cross from Oronsay, marking the grave of Bishop Chinnery-Haldane, who died in 1906 (Fig. 36).

5.27 Onich
NN 031 614: OS 41

The Parliamentary church was replaced by the present building, designed by Alexander Ross, in 1875, but the Parliamentary manse (now a private house) survives beside it, though with bay windows added later (NN 031 614)

Fig. 37. St Margaret's Roman Catholic Church, Roybridge (5.29)

5.28 Polnish, Lochailort   NM 751 827: OS 40

A Roman Catholic church built in 1874 in an isolated position, designed to be visible from Inverailort House. Now disused.

5.29 Roybridge, St Margaret's Roman Catholic Church
(Fig. 37)   NN 270 814: OS 41

A fine building by Reginald Fairlie, complete with adjoining Presbytery House

5.30 Spean Bridge, Kilmonivaig Parish Church
                                       NN 212 819: OS 41

Built in 1812, altered in 1891 by Alexander Ross, and again in 1928. It contains some good twentieth-century stained glass. Its medieval predecessor was down by the river Lochy, near its junction with the Spean, possibly at NN 173 838, or at Gairlochy, but there are now no visible remains of either church or burial ground.

5.31 Strontian, Parliamentary Church
                                       NM 815 624: OS 40

Built in 1827–9, but altered in 1924. Although there are some burials around the Parliamentary church, the present graveyard is an

Fig. 38. View of the old graveyard at Strontian, the central mound presumably covering the remains of the former church (5.31)

extension of the earlier one (NM 819 626: OS 40), where graves have been set on a mound which presumably incorporates the remains of the pre-1827 church (Fig. 38).

West Highland Museum

Among the exhibits are a late-medieval grave slab from Kilmallie churchyard; the bell from the old Maryburgh church, built in 1790; an iron cage from the graveyard in Glen Nevis, designed to protect new burials from the grave robbers looking for fresh bodies to sell to anatomy students; and a panel from the Floating Church on Loch Sunart (Fig. 8).

6. COUNTRY HOUSES

The Highlands are not rich in domestic architecture. (Compton Mackenzie, *Hunting the Fairies*, 1949)

6.1   Achnacarry (Fig. 39)   NN 176 879: OS 41

Described by the *Ordnance Gazetteer* as 'One of the loveliest of Highland seats', is where the Camerons of Locheil settled after they abandoned Tor Castle (4.12) in 1665. The first house was destroyed in the aftermath of Culloden in 1746, and the estate forfeited. The lands were restored to the family in 1784, but work on the castellated Gothic mansion designed by James Gillespie Graham did not begin until 1802. James Hogg, the Ettrick Shepherd, visited in 1803 and saw the new house being built. He described James Gillespie Graham as 'a respectable young man, possessed of much professional knowledge'. The old castle had been 'reduced to ashes by the Duke of Cumberland's forces . . . and the marks of the fire are still too visible, not only on the remaining walls of the house and offices, but also on a number of huge venerable trees, which the malevolent brutes had kindled'.

Fig. 39. Achnacarry House (6.1)

The Locheil who started the rebuilding lost enthusiasm, and left the house incomplete. When Joseph Mitchell visited in 1837 he noted that 'the plaster ornaments of the ceiling lay all that time on the floor ready to be fixed, and the doors of the rooms, of beautiful Highland pine grown brown with age, leaned against the walls ready to be screwed on. They had remained in this position for thirty-five years.' The next Locheil completed the house. In February 1942 Achnacarry became the headquarters for commando basic training. Damaged by fire during the war, it was restored in 1952. The Clan Cameron Museum stands in its grounds. (Private, not visible from road, but can be seen by walking a short distance from the Clan Cameron Museum.)

6.2 Ardgour House   NM 995 638: OS 40

A plain Georgian mansion built for the Macleans of Ardgour in 1765. Gutted by fire in 1825, it was restored and enlarged by Alexander Squair in 1826–30, adding a portico and two-storey wings for Colonel Alexander Maclean, who had made money in India. The local minister in 1835 described it as 'surrounded by planting and shrubbery laid out with great taste'. (Private, not visible from the road.)

6.3 Ardtornish (Plate 21)   NM 703 475: OS 49

A large Victorian house at the head of Loch Aline. The first house was built between 1856 and 1866 for Octavius Smith, but demolished in 1884 by his son Valentine (except for the clock-tower, Fig. 40) and replaced by the present house built between 1885 and 1891. Designed by Alexander Ross of Inverness, it is built of concrete with stone facing on the west and south fronts, along with a glass-roofed veranda with cast-iron columns. The interior was neo-Jacobean, surviving mainly around the main staircase. Much of the interior was redesigned in 1908–10 by John Kinross, imitating a variety of eighteenth-century styles. Near the house is a wide range of ancillary buildings, from

Fig. 40. The clock tower, all that remains of the first Ardtornish House, 1855–66 (6.3)

vast barns to kennels and a weighbridge. (Private, but visible, and the gardens are open to the public.)

6.4   Arisaig House   NM 691 848: OS 40

In the 1860s the new owner of the estate, Mr Astley, abandoned the old Arisaig House (now Borrodale farmhouse) and built on a new site to a design by Philip Webb, 'in the French villa style, and consequently ill-suited to a Highland climate' (Joseph Mitchell). This burned down in 1935, and was replaced by an Arts and Crafts house built in 1936–7. The south-east wing is all that remains of the

1860s house. Arisaig House served as a base for Special Operations Executive training during the Second World War. (Private, visible from the road when travelling west.)

6.5   Ballachulish House   NN 047 592 : OS 41

The seat of the Stewarts of Ballachulish. The main block is of two storeys. The east part is the oldest, dating from about 1764 (a lintel with this date has been rebuilt in a bothy nearby), with the western part added in about 1799. The two-storeyed north wing and south kitchen wing of one storey and garret were added in the first half of the nineteenth century. (Now a hotel.)

6.6   Borrodale House   NM 694 850 : OS 40

Where Bonnie Prince Charlie stayed when he first landed, and returned after Culloden. Angus MacDonald of Borrodale's wife was said to have made him a suit of Highland clothes so that he could travel incognito. The old house was burnt in reprisal in 1746, but subsequently rebuilt, possibly on the same site. It now looks top-heavy, having had large dormer windows added. It is now a farmhouse, having been replaced by Arisaig House. (Private, but visible from the road.)

6.7   Callert House, Loch Leven   NN 091 604 : OS 41

A laird's house with recessed wings, built 1835–37 for Sir Duncan Cameron. Additions were made in about 1900. 'It stands close to the seashore, surrounded by trees and green fields, and commanding in every direction a far-spread view of sea and mountains' (Joseph Mitchell, 1883). In the grounds is the Cameron mausoleum (NN 071 598). To the west, across the stream, stands a low platform (NN 092 603), all that remains of the earlier house, said to have been deliberately burned in about 1640 because of an outbreak of plague brought by a visiting Spanish ship. In the West Highland Museum is a carved oak settle from Callert House. (Private, but visible from the road.)

6.8   Dalelia (Plate 23)   NM 733 693: OS 40

Built in about 1800 for Alexander MacDonald, a banker, who added a new front to an older house. The house was altered in 1907 in the Scots Baronial style for Lord Howard of Glossop, with the addition of a top floor, turrets and crowsteps. (Private, but close to and visible from the road to the pier.)

6.9   Drimnin   NM 553 550: OS 47

Built in the 1850s for Sir Charles Gordon, replacing a house which burnt down in 1849. The steading was also built at this time. The interior retains much of its original decoration, including fine painted-marble stair and hall walls, and painted panels in the drawing rooms. (Private, visible from footpath.)

6.10   Errocht House, Glen Loy   NN 142 823: OS 41

A farmhouse, once the home of the Camerons of Erracht, and (the ground floor at least) standing in 1715.

6.11   Fassfern House, on the north shore of Loch Eil
NN 021 787: OS 41

One of the very few houses not burned down in 1746. When Joseph Mitchell visited in the mid nineteenth century he described it as 'a fair specimen of a Highland country gentleman's farm residence sixty or seventy years since – doors and shutters of original pine unpainted, and the paper on the walls bearing evidence of the moisture of the Lochaber climate'. It was the home of Colonel John Cameron (1771–1815), who died at Quatre Bras and is commemorated by an obelisk below Kilmallie parish church at Corpach. (Private, just visible from main road.)

6.12   Glenborrodale Castle, Ardnamurchan
NM 606 608: OS 40

On the hillside on the north shore of Loch Sunart, built 1898–1902 in the baronial style for C.M. Rudd, the then Laird of Ardnamurchan. In 1935 it was bought by Jesse Boot, Lord Trent. When he sold in 1949 the whole estate of Ardnamurchan was broken up. The house is constructed of Dumfriesshire red sandstone, by the same builder as the Western Isles Hotel in Tobermory. (Now a hotel.)

6.13   Glencoe House
NN 103 595: OS 41

On the lower slopes of the Pap of Glencoe, was built as a shooting lodge for Donald Smith, of the Hudson Bay Company and the Canadian Pacific Railway. He bought the estate of Glencoe from the MacDonalds in 1893, and had the house built, to designs by Robert Rowand Anderson, in 1896–7, by which time he had been created Lord Strathcona. It is constructed of grey granite with red sandstone dressings, and crowstepped gables. When the National Trust for Scotland bought the estate in 1935, the house was bought by Argyll County Council for use as a maternity home. In 1965 it was reduced in size by the demolition of the two wings. (Now a hospital.)

6.14   Glengarry Castle (formerly Invergarry House)
NH 316 010: OS 34

The estate of Glengarry was bought in 1860 by Edward Ellice of Glenquoich (1810–80), from 1837 to 1880 MP for the St Andrews burghs. He built here in 1866–8 a baronial house designed by David Bryce, with a stable block added in 1875-6. (Now a hotel.)

6.15   Inverailort House   NM 763 815: OS 40

A Georgian farmhouse converted to a shooting lodge by the
construction of baronial additions at both ends in 1875 and 1891. It
was used as a base for commando units during the Second World
War. (Private, but close to the road.)

6.16   Inverlochy Castle (Torlundy) (Plate 22)
NN 138 767: OS 41

Two miles north of old Inverlochy Castle, a castellated house built
in 1860–63 by Lord Abinger, with uninspired additions in 1889–92.
Or, in the words of the *Ordnance Gazetteer* of 1894, 'partly in the
Scottish Baronial style . . . partly a large ornate modern villa, with
a round central flag-tower, and a massive square porticoed tower at
the principal entrance'. Queen Victoria stayed here for a week in 1873.
The wet weather put her off buying Ardverikie, on Loch Laggan,
and she later bought Balmoral instead. (Now a hotel.)

6.17   Keppoch House, Arisaig   NM 655 867: OS 40

Built in about 1800 for Alexander MacDonald of Glenaladale, father
of the man who built the Glenfinnan Monument (12.5). A two-storey
main block with single-storey wings, the right hand wing originally
a byre.

6.18   Keppoch House, Roybridge   NN 268 809: OS 34

The seat of the Macdonnells of Keppoch. The first house was built
in the early sixteenth century by the sixth Macdonnell of Keppoch,
on a mound (probably natural) at the confluence of the rivers Roy
and Spean (NN 270 807), surrounded by a moat. After 1663 it
was deliberately destroyed, and nothing remains. A second house
was burned down in 1746, and the present one built in about 1760.
(Private, not visible from the road.)

6.19 Kinlochmoidart House NM 716 723: OS 40

The first house, where Bonnie Prince Charlie stayed, was burned down in 1746. It was replaced by a small house, which survives behind the present one. Enlarged by Colonel Robertson and then by his son, the house was then replaced by a late Victorian Scots Baronial house, built in 1885 by William Leiper for Robert Stewart of Ingliston, a distiller, to a design almost identical to his villa at Helensburgh. It is built of whinstone, with red sandstone dressings, and crowsteps. The west lodge is of the same date, and the steading slightly older. (Private, can be glimpsed from the road, and from the surrounding hills.)

6.20 Letterfinlay (Fig. 41) NN 253 914: OS 34

Said to have been built by General Wade's soldiers as officers' quarters (or as an inn to house them), beside the road along the east side of Loch Lochy. It later became a drovers' inn (where many men fleeing from Culloden took refuge and some died), then the mansion of the Letterfinlay estate, until the present Letterfinlay Lodge was built in the late nineteenth century. (Private, but right beside the road.)

Fig. 41. Early eighteenth-century house at Letterfinlay, beside Loch Lochy (6.20)

6.21 Mamore Lodge, Loch Leven   NN 185 629: OS 41

Six hundred feet (200 m) up the hillside above Kinlochleven, near the old military road, was built as a shooting lodge, one of many erected in the Highlands in the nineteenth century. (Now a hotel, and visible from the road on the south side of the loch.)

6.22 Roshven   NM 705 788: OS 40

A late Georgian laird's house, bought in 1855 as a holiday home by Hugh Blackburn, Professor of Mathematics at Glasgow University, and his artist wife Jemima. The house was rebuilt to designs by David Bryce in 1857–9, and altered further in 1896, using the concrete whose qualities were being exploited for the viaducts on the West Highland Railway at this time. The house was only accessible by sea or on foot until the building of the Kinlochmoidart to Lochailort road in 1966. (Private, not visible from the road.)

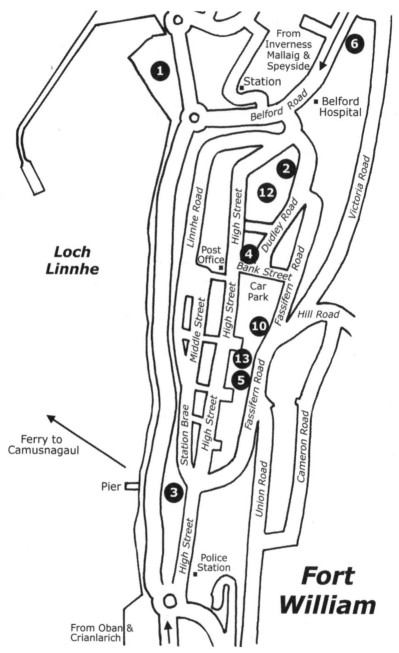

Map. 2. Fort William, with the main town centre features marked with their gazetteer numbers

7. FORT WILLIAM
(OS 41, AND EXPLORER SHEET 392)

Key buildings are marked with their numbers on Map 2.

7.1   The Fort (Figs 10 and 42)   **NN 104 742**

Parts of the north and west ramparts survive, and the north-west demi-bastion. The simpler stonework along the loch side probably dates from 1690, whereas the coursed masonry is probably eighteenth century. The sea-gate within this later wall is shown on a plan of the fort in 1656. One 1690 gateway was re-erected at the Craigs Burial

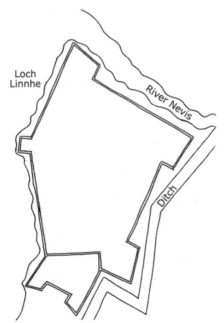

Fig. 42. Plan of the Cromwellian fort at Inverlochy, built in 1656, rebuilt 1690 and renamed Fort William (7.1)

Ground (originally created to serve the fort) (NN 108 742) (Plate 8) in 1896. Although now cut off from the town by the shore road, and with little obvious to attract the visitor, the remains of the fort are worth exploring.

Churches

7.2   Duncansburgh Parish Church

The main town-centre church, Maryburgh church, in Cameron Square, was built in 1790. In 1881 it was replaced, and was subsequently used as the Town Hall, but burned down in 1975. Its replacement, Duncansburgh Parish Church, out at the north end of the town, was built in 1881, paid for by Sir Duncan Cameron of Fassifern.

7.3   Free Church

At the south end of the High Street, a simple but attractive building of 1846 (Fig. 43)

Fig. 43. The Free Church, Fort William (7.3)

7.4   St Andrews Episcopal Church, High Street.

The site was given by the War Office in 1817, and a small chapel was built. In 1879–84 it was replaced by the present pink granite church, designed by Alexander Ross of Inverness. Described by one traveller as 'one of the most beautiful on the West coast', it perhaps has less appeal to modern observers, though it has a fine interior, with carved wooden doors, and high-quality stained glass and furnishings, including Minton tiles and an Italian mosaic floor. The associated rectory was demolished in 1958.

7.5   Mackintosh Memorial Church, Fassifern Road

Built in 1887–90, up on the hill

7.6   The Church of the Immaculate Conception

The Roman Catholic church designed by Reginald Fairlie and built in 1933–4, replacing an earlier building of 1868. A strong and simple design, its impact is slightly spoiled by its position so close to the main road north.

7.7   St Mary's Church

Later Macrae and Dick's garage, Station Square, now offices

Other buildings of interest or quality

7.8   Sheriff Court

Built in 1876

7.9   St Andrews House, Fassifern Road

Built in 1880 as the Episcopal school, designed by Alexander Ross (and one of his more successful designs)

7.10   Obelisk, Fassifern Road

Erected in 1847 by Sir Duncan Cameron of Fassifern in memory of his brother, Captain Peter Cameron, commander of the East Indiaman *The Earl of Balcarres*

7.11   Belford Hospital

The first hospital here was established in 1864 by Andrew Belford of Glenfintaig, in a building donated to the town in his will, for the benefit of the poorer classes of the parishes of Kilmallie and Kilmonivaig. It was described by Queen Victoria in 1873 as 'a neat building'. The old hospital was demolished in the early 1960s and the present one opened in 1965.

7.12   Parade Ground

The public open space at the north end of the High Street was once the parade ground of the Fort. It is overlooked by the former Governor's House (NN 104 740), built in the early eighteenth century, with a nineteenth-century wing added to the right. Within the parade ground stand:

War memorial, *c.*1920

Statue of Donald Cameron of Locheil, twenty-fourth chief of Clan Cameron (d.1905), erected in 1909

Peace monument, 1985, incorporating the bellcote of the old parish church, later the town hall

7.13   West Highland Museum

Built *c.*1840 for the British Linen Bank. Inside, mid eighteenth-century panelling from the Governor's House of the Fort.

7.14 The High Street

Contains a mix of architecture of the nineteenth and twentieth centuries, constructed in a wide range of materials, including pink granite, grey granite, and red sandstone, but little that is memorable.

Bank of Scotland, *c.*1860

Royal Bank, formerly National Bank, 1911

Masonic Hall, 1903

38 High Street, built as British Linen Bank *c.*1860, now McIntyre & Co.

Ossian Hotel, formerly Stag's Head Hotel, and originally Palace Hotel, late Victorian, red sandstone

Queen Anne House, half-timbered, 111–115 High St, *c.*1900

7.15 Highland Hotel

Formerly the Railway Hotel, built 1895, in Union Road, overlooking the south end of the High Street (NN 101 736). It served as naval local HQ during the Second World War.

7.16 Alexandra Hotel

Beside the parish church, overlooking the north end of the Parade Ground, built in 1876

7.17 The low level observatory, Achintore Road

Built of red sandstone in 1889, for collecting weather data (Plate 24). Like the observatory on the top of Ben Nevis, it went out of use in 1904, and is now a private house.

8. SITES RELATING TO
THE RURAL ECONOMY

Throughout the area the observant traveller will notice former areas of arable cultivation, still showing the rig and furrow profile. One can also see sections of turf dyke, and identify different styles of dry-stone dyking. Most isolated settlements ground corn by hand. The eighteenth century saw a few water-driven mills, but it was not until the nineteenth century that many were built, mostly in association with the larger estates. Barns have the distinctive Highland feature of slits in the walls which allow ventilation without letting in rain.

Farm and Estate Buildings

8.1 Achnacarry   NN 175 877: OS 34

The Clan Cameron Museum is housed in a pair of large but old and solid cottages, perhaps once used by estate staff. There is also a large courtyard of nineteenth-century estate buildings, in poor repair, to the south of the house (Fig. 44).

8.2 Achranich, now Ardtornish   NM 704 473: OS 49

A collection of estate and farm buildings including a vast barn (or wool store) built in 1851 (Fig. 14). From the 1870s building changed from stone to concrete, including a coach house range of 1871–2 (possibly the first concrete building in Scotland), the Estate Office and Factor's House (1880), and an early twentieth-century power station. Other distinctive concrete buildings can be found all over the estate (Plate 26).

Fig. 44. Steading and estate offices, Achnacarry (8.1)

8.3   Ardtornish   NM 692 432: OS 49

A late eighteenth- or early nineteenth-century steading associated with Old Ardtornish House (now demolished)

8.4   Arisaig   NM 659 866: OS 40

A nice barn at the top of the village

8.5   Borrodale Farm, Arisaig   NM 694 850: OS 40

1864 steading designed by Philip Webb, with a very large barn, built into the hillside, right beside the road

8.6   Drimnin, Morvern   NM 559 538: OS 47

The ruins of Mungasdail Mill, occupied by 1744, out of use by 1882. In the later eighteenth century it was one of three mills in Morvern parish.

8.7   Invergarry   NH 296 012: OS 34

Corn mill, *c.*1800

8.8   Keppoch House, Roybridge   NN 269 809: OS 34

A large barn in traditional style (Fig. 45), and other buildings

Fig. 45. Large barn at Keppoch House, Roybridge (8.8)

8.9 Kinlochmoidart, Low Farm (Fig. 46) NM 707 727: OS 40

A large mid nineteenth-century courtyard of farm buildings right on the road.

8.10 Drumnatorra Farm, Strontian NM 820 625: OS 40

Has a large, though derelict, steading, at the centre of some good land, and just across the burn from the old church site. It was described in 1838 as a 'well-managed farm and excellent farm-house and offices'.

Sites associated with fishing

8.11 Fascadale Bay, Ardnamurchan NM 500 707: OS 47

Ice house for a salmon fishing station

8.12 Mallaig NM 677 972: OS 40

Created after the coming of the railway in 1901, as a fishing port. 'The town . . . leaves much to be desired, both in lay-out and architecture' (MacCulloch, *Romantic Lochaber*).

8.13 North Tarbet NM 791 923: OS 40

A fishing village on Loch Nevis, abandoned after Mallaig was founded and a pier built there

Fig. 46. Low Farm, Kinlochmoidart (8.9)

Fish-traps can be found on a number of beaches, often in out-of-the-way places. Sometimes their presence is indicated by the place name. Port na Cairidh, at the western end of Ardnamurchan, means 'port of the fish-trap'. Those visible from the road include:

8.14 Camas Shallachain, Ardgour   NM 987 622: OS 40

A rectilinear trap at the outer end of the bay

8.15 Killundine, Morvern   NM 584 487: OS 47

A fish-trap with two angular arms enclosing a small bay

8.16 Rubha na h'Airde Seiliche, north of Kingairloch
                                    NM 883 538: OS 49

A semicircular stone fish-trap close to the road (Plate 20; Fig. 47)

Cleared settlements

Abandoned clusters of cottages can be found all over the area, and are often marked on OS maps. The main forced clearances took place during the first half of the nineteenth century, but there are earlier and later examples as well.

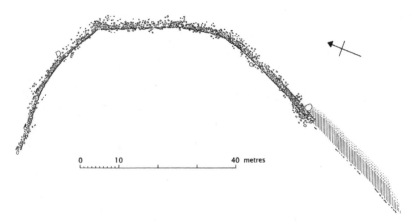

Fig. 47. Plan of the stone fish-trap near Kingairloch (Colin Martin) (8.16)

8.17   Ardnish peninsula, west of Lochailort

Was cleared in 1940 to allow the training of commandos

8.18   Auliston   NM 549 571: OS 47

The largest cleared village in Morvern, and not buried in bracken. Over 100 people were evicted in 1855. There is a lower section at 547 577.

8.19   Bourblaige, Ardnamurchan   NM 546 622. OS 47

Consisting of about thirty-five buildings, was abandoned by 1829

8.20   Camas nan Geall, Ardnamurchan (Plate 19)
NM 559 618: OS 47

A sheltered bay with ruined cottages and a graveyard. Accessible by a track from a car park and viewpoint on the main road. A typical small area of good land on the coast, enclosed by hills. There is another settlement a little way up the valley, overlooking the bay, at 556 622.

8.21 Inniemore, Morvern   NM 655 518: OS 49

A large settlement cleared in 1824, rediscovered by the Forestry Commission when felling trees. It is now accessible via a network of paths leading from the car park at NM 667 517.

8.22 Plocaig, Ardnamurchan   NM 453 697: OS 47

Abandoned in the early twentieth century

8.23 Swordle, Ardnamurchan   NM 54 70: OS 40

Three communities here were cleared in the 1850s, and their tenants resettled in Sanna and Portuairk (NM 44 69). This meant a ten-hour journey on foot, as many times as was necessary to transport not only household possessions but stocks such as potatoes.

8.24 Uladail, Morvern (Figs 12 and 13)   NM 716 506: OS 49

Just above the A884, consists of about 16 houses and a corn-drying kiln. It seems to have been cleared around 1840, just before it was sold to Patrick Sellar. Some of the houses are older, as they are not marked on an estate map of 1833. Some of the arable fields belonging to the settlement lay between the present road and the river, and rig-and-furrow can still be seen.

Crofting townships

In contrast with the jumbled layout of the deserted settlements, there are some clusters of houses which have been deliberately laid out in a line, with a long strip of land belonging to each cottage. These are the crofting settlements mostly created during the nineteenth century. Those beside main roads include the back of Glencoe village, North Ballachulish (as you drive west off the bridge, there are fields to your left running down to the shore, while among the modern houses to your right can be seen the remains of little cottages, built end on to the road), the back of Clovullin (as one drives into Ardnamurchan from the Corran ferry), at the west end of Kilchoan, and at Back of Keppoch, north of Arisaig. Others can be found by looking at maps.

Newer settlements and planned villages

8.25 Annat   NN 08 77/78: OS 41

Built at the beginning of the Second World War for families of those posted to the small naval base at Corpach. It later became a suburb of Fort William, as have Banavie and Corpach.

8.26 Banavie   NN 11 77: OS 41

Created for workers on the Caledonian Canal

8.27 Glencoe village   NN 10 58: OS 41

Was created in the late eighteenth century, when the upper part of the glen was cleared for sheep

8.28 Invergarry   NH 30 01: OS 34

A planned village, built in the 1860s and 1870s, with rustic porches on the cottages

8.29 Kinlochleven   NN 18/19 61/62: OS 41

Built for workers at the aluminium smelter established at the head of Loch Leven in 1909

8.30 Larachbeg, Morvern   NM 694 483: OS 49

A row of six concrete cottages built for workers on the Ardtornish estate in 1875, and used in the 1930s to house families evacuated from St Kilda

8.31 Lochaline, Morvern   NM 67 44: OS 49

First laid out in about 1830 by John Sinclair of Lochaline. The surviving older buildings mostly date to the late nineteenth or early twentieth century.

Mallaig (see above 8.12)

8.32 Strontian   NM 81 61: OS 40

A 1960s model village built by the Highlands and Islands Development Board around a green, on a site owned by the government

Schools

Early schools were often held in churches, or in the schoolmaster's house. Purpose-built schools were not usually constructed until the second half of the nineteenth century. These are distinctive because of their high ceilings, showing concern about airborne infection, deliberately contrasting with earlier cramped and low-ceilinged buildings. Many have since been replaced, or become redundant as the population has fallen.

8.33 Roybridge   NN 272 810: OS 41

A good surviving example of a Victorian school

Village Halls

Mostly dating from some time in the twentieth century, few are of much interest. Several, as at Duror (Kentallen), and Kilchoan, have been replaced during the past decade.

8.34 Arisaig, Astley Hall (Fig. 48)   NM 662 864: OS 40

Designed by Philip Webb, and built in 1893, presumably paid for by the owners of Arisaig House

Fig. 48. Astley Hall, Arisaig (8.34)

8.35 Mingarry   NM 686 694: OS 40

A typical small hall built of corrugated iron

8.36 Onich, Nether Lochaber Village Hall   NN 046 611: OS 41

Another typical corrugated-iron hall

West Highland Museum

Objects on display include agricultural tools, an illicit still, and a range of domestic items.

9. INDUSTRIAL SITES

9.1   Ironworks and the production and supply of charcoal

There is nothing to see at the site of the Glengarry ironworks. In almost any area of broad-leafed woodland, however, you may come across circular platforms which were built or adapted for the burning of charcoal. Near Loch Etive, for example, various charcoal-burning stances survive above the pier at the head of the loch, and between Kinlochetive and Inverliever. Some at least are related to the establishment of the ironworks in Glen Kinglass (which closed in the 1730s), while charcoal from the Sunart woodlands and even further away was supplying the ironworks at Bonawe, near Taynuilt. **Bonawe** (NN 010 319: OS 50), while outside Lochaber, is well worth a visit.

Lead-mining

9.2   Lurga, Morvern   NM 778 596: OS 49

The site of the lead-mines at **Lurga**, in Liddesdale, across Loch Sunart from Strontian, can be visited on foot. There are remains of open-cast workings (NM 732 554) and ruined buildings, perhaps dating from a brief revival of the workings in 1803 (NM 735 553). The most prominent remains, however, are on the shore, where in 1733 the company had 'built a hansome dwelling house for their Manager, Clerks and Office at Liedgesdale, besides a Key with a compleat Storehouse, upon it, two Warehouses, Lodging houses for workmen, two large Stables and as many Barns, a Malt Kiln, a Smith's chop and Workhouse'.

9.3   Strontian   NM 80-88 66: OS 40

Up the valley running north from Strontian are two lead seams, accessed at various places including Corantee (NM 804 658), Free Donald (NM 863 665), Bellsgroove (NM 837 657), Middleshope (NM 831 654) and Whitesmith (NM 833 657), the last three visible from the road from Strontian to Polloch. If you explore away from the road you will come across a lot of evidence of industrial activity, some obvious in its purpose, some less so.

Copper-mining

9.4   Loch Tearnait   NM 765 478: OS 49

Copper was mined and smelted in the eighteenth century in Morvern, east of Loch Tearnait, where spoil heaps and a water-filled shaft are visible and slag is found. The mine appears to have been in use at the time of Roy's survey (1747–55) but abandoned by 1794.

Silica sand mining

9.5   Lochaline   NM 680 448: OS 49

To quote the minister of Morvern in 1954, 'In 1925 Sir Edward Bailey of the Geological Survey drew attention to the value of a bed of white cretaceous sandstone . . . some 18 feet in thickness and appeared suitable for the manufacture of high quality glass . . . in 1940 mining operations began. This was opportune, for the mine was the only source of supply in Great Britain of sand suitable for making optical and other glass required for the war effort'. It is still working, and the sand is wholly exported by sea.

Quarries

9.6   Ballachulish slate quarries   NN 08 58: OS 41

The Tourist Information Centre in Ballachulish has a display on the slate industry. Remains include a few of the original houses, built in the eighteenth century for 72 families (NN 075, 585). The quarries themselves are at West Laroch and East Laroch. Both had harbours, constructed from quarry waste. The larger quarry, East Laroch, has a path laid out inside it, with seats and information boards (park at the Tourist Information Centre). There is also a path up the west side of the quarry, from the top of which there are fine views.

9.7 Brunachan, Glen Roy   NN 31 89: OS 41

A quarry from which quernstones were transported or traded as far as the Outer Isles

9.8 Inninmore, on the south coast of Morvern
NM 725 418: OS 49

Was a source of sandstone. On the foreshore are the traces of millstone cutting, and waster gravestones.

9.9 Kentallen   NN 022 590: OS 41

Former granite quarries

9.10 Kingairloch   NM 851 526: OS 49

Former granite quarry, and pier for shipping it out

Aluminium smelting

9.11 Inverlochy aluminium smelter   NN 126 750: OS 41

Opened in 1931, it was powered by water from Loch Treig (there is a small display on the aluminium industry in the West Highland Museum, Fort William). The massive pipes carrying the water down to the works dominate the northern suburbs of Fort William.

9.12   Laggan Dam (Fig. 17)   NN 372 807: OS 41

Built in 1934, as part of the system powering the Inverlochy aluminium works

9.13   Kinlochleven aluminium smelter   NN 188 618: OS 41

Opened in 1909, and was extended in the 1930s, when much of the housing was built. The works closed in 2000. The water power came from the Blackwater dam. There is a Visitor Centre, 'The Aluminium Story', recording the history of the industry.

Distilleries

9.14   Ben Nevis Distillery, Fort William   NN 125 757: OS 41

Was established in 1825 by 'Long John' MacDonald of Keppoch, and is still working. The Nevis distillery was founded as an extension to the Ben Nevis distillery. It closed in 1908, though its buildings remained in use as warehouses until the 1980s, but have since been demolished.

9.15   Glenlochy Distillery, North Road, Fort William
NN 112 743: OS 41

Built in 1898–1900, at the height of prosperity and confidence in the distilling industry, and its architecture is therefore distinctive. It closed in 1983, but its maltings with their typical roofs survive.

10. TRANSPORT AND COMMUNICATIONS

MARITIME TRANSPORT

Harbours and landing places of all types and of all periods can be found along the shores of Lochaber, and piers on inland lochs. Many, including those still in use, are marked on OS maps. Piers changed in design as shipping changed. Simple piers or quays sufficed for a long time. The amount of top surface area needed depended on what was being shipped in and out. As few people had wheeled vehicles, most piers and quays were only wide enough for cattle. A quarry pier might be much larger than one handling passengers.

Early piers

Solid, flat-topped stone piers or quays began to be built during the first half of the nineteenth century, in some cases to provide work during the potato famine, or generally by landowners to boost the local economy.

10.1   Lochaline Old Pier, Morvern   NM 679 446: OS 49

Built in 1848

10.2   Salen Pier, Ardnamurchan   NM 688 642: OS 40

Built in the 1830s

Steamer piers

Steamers, however, required piers in positions which did not require them to turn more than necessary. And as timetables became more important, piers had to be accessible even at low water. So new structures were built on new sites. Redundant steamer piers can be seen in a number of places, in prominent positions. They were often built of wood, and all that now remains is massive stumps.

10.3 Ballachulish Pier   NN 038 595: OS 41

With an associated pier house across the road

10.4 Kinlochmoidart (Plate 25)   NM 696 728: OS 40

A typical example, with a stone pier extended with wooden posts

10.5 Lochaline, Morvern   NM 683 442: OS 49

The West Pier was built for steamers in 1883, complete with concrete piermaster's house and post office, built in 1898–9

Ferries

Early ferries may have had no built infrastructure, but later ones usually leave some evidence, perhaps a simple construction of boulders to tidy up the natural rock features and help landing at all states of the tide. Major ferry points often had an inn or 'change house'. Such sites are often indicated by the place-name 'Doirlinn'.

10.6 Ballachulish   NN 051 596; 053 597: OS 41

The old ferry slips can be seen beneath the bridge

10.7 Corran Narrows   NN 016 637; 021 635: OS 41

Between Nether Lochaber and Ardgour, a long-established ferry, served by ever-larger vessels and very busy

10.8 Doirlinn, Loch Moidart   NM 662 718: OS 40

10.9 Doirlinn, Loch Sunart   NM 606 585: OS 49

At the west end of Morvern (now only accessible on foot), from where a ferry used to run to Ardnamurchan

10.10 Lochaline   NM 679 446; 681 447: OS 49

A pair of piers on either side of the narrows at the entrance to Loch Aline for a ferry serving Ardtornish

Boathouses

Most maritime transport was privately owned, and many landowners built boathouses for their private boats (Plate 21). Many of these can be seen marked on the 1:25,000 maps, as for example several around Loch Moidart and Kentra Bay. They are plain buildings, generally of stone, but sometimes of wood, but reflecting estate architecture rather than the vernacular tradition. Those visible from the road include:

10.11 Fiunary, Morvern   NM 623 461: OS 49

Simple stone boathouse

10.12 Glencoe   NN 102 599: OS 41

Stone boathouse now converted into a house

Lighthouses

10.13 Ardnamurchan Point (Fig. 49)   NM 415 674: OS 47

The most westerly point of the British mainland, it was the worst danger to mariners between Cape Wrath and the Mull of Kintyre. Therefore a lighthouse was built there in 1846–9, designed by Alan Stevenson, at a cost of £13,738. It is 114 feet high, with its light 180 ft above sea level. It became automatic in 1988, and its buildings are now a museum.

Fig. 49. Lighthouse at Ardnamurchan Point (10.13)

10.14 Corran Narrows   NN 017 635: OS 41

A low lighthouse, built by D. & T. Stevenson in 1860, with a pair of keeper's houses, and a brick store of about the same date

Caledonian Canal

10.15 Aberchalder, at the north end of Loch Oich
NH 337 037: OS 34

There is a lock-keeper's cottage, and a suspension bridge built in 1850 by James Dredge of Bath (and its modern replacement built in 1930–2)

Fig. 50. Neptune's Staircase, Banavie (from Anon., Mountain Moor and Loch, 1894) (10.16)

10.16 Banavie, Neptune's Staircase (Fig. 50) NN 113 769: OS 41

A flight of eight locks, built between 1807 and 1811
A railway swing bridge, constructed in 1901   NN 113 770: OS 41

10.17 Corpach, locks   NN 095 766: OS 41

Lock-keeper's cottages   NN 097 766: OS 41
A little lighthouse at the entrance to the canal, built in 1913
                                         NN 095 766: OS 41

10.18 Gairlochy   NN 181 846: OS 41

Locks, and lock-keeper's cottages, with stables behind, built originally to house those working on the canal. The middle room upstairs, with its bay window, is known as 'Telford's Room', as he stayed here on visits to inspect the work.

10.19 Laggan   NN 285 962: OS 34

Locks

Swing bridge   NN 300 983: OS 34

10.20 Moy   NN 162 826: OS 34

The only surviving original cast-iron swing bridge

ROADS AND BRIDGES

The area has a number of paths, some of which will be of great antiquity. Corpach and Onich were traditional sites for the embarkation of funeral parties of the elite who were buried on Iona. For others, coffin roads led to traditional burial isles, the main ones being Eileann Finnan in Loch Shiel and Eilean Munde in Loch Leven. A network of coffin roads crosses Ardnamurchan and Moidart to converge on Loch Shiel and the various piers from which funeral parties could embark. Along these roads coffin cairns may be found, where the funeral party rested. The 1:25,000 series of maps marks some of the these tracks and cairns.

10.21 Cill Choirille   NN 302/3 809/900: OS 41

Cairns

10.22 General Robertson's Cairn (Plate 17) NM 731 714: OS 40

On the road over the hill from Kinlochmoidart to Dalelia

10.23 Glencoe   NN 188 562: OS 41

Coffin cairn. There were also tracks along which pedlars and others travelled with pack ponies. There were very few wheeled vehicles before the nineteenth century, so the first need for wider, solider roads was to move troops effectively.

Wade roads and bridges, 1725–33

The road from Fort William to Inverness, along the Great Glen, left Fort William through Craigs Burial Ground. It rejoined the present road at NN 207 844, on the A82 at the Commando Monument. Many sections are marked on OS maps. On the east shore of Loch Oich some of the Wade Road may be under the old railway line.

10.24 High Bridge (Plate 13)   NN 200 821: OS 41

Built in 1736/7, it was last repaired in 1893. In about 1913 the south arch collapsed; by 1979 only one arch survived, and that too has now fallen. There is a cairn beside the road (NN 199 818), from which a path leads to the bridge.

10.25 Low Bridge   NN 224 864: OS 41

Built across the River Gloy *c.*1726

Caulfield Roads, from 1750

The military road from Stirling to Fort William is followed by the West Highland Way between Rannoch and Kinlochleven, including the Devil's Staircase, and on over Lairig Mor towards Fort William.

Parliamentary Roads, 1803–23

These include the road from Spean Bridge to Newtonmore, on which stands

10.26 Spean Bridge (Fig. 51)   NN 221 816: OS 41

Built in 1813, and widened in 1932, replacing Wade's High Bridge

Fig. 51. Old Spean Bridge (from Anon., Mountain Moor and Loch, 1894) (10.26)

Another Parliamentary road, started in 1804, runs from Ardgour to Inverailort. Surviving bridges on it include:

10.27 Ardmolich Bridge, Kinlochmoidart   NM 713 721: OS 40

10.28 Old Shiel Bridge, Acharacle, on the site of Torquil's Ford
NM 674 692: OS 40

10.29 Salachan Bridge, near Ardgour   NM 978 629: OS 40

Later bridges

10.30 Aberchalder   NH 337 036: OS 34
A Victorian suspension bridge at the head of Loch Oich, built in 1850 (Fig. 52)

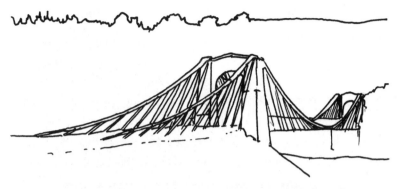

Fig. 52. Suspension Bridge, Aberchalder, Loch Oich (10.30)

10.31 Ballachulish Bridge   NN 052 597/8: OS 41

Built in 1975, replacing the ferry (and thereby taking traffic and trade away from Kinlochleven, as the ferry queues were so long that many drivers took the longer route around the loch).

10.32 Shiel Bridge   NM 677 689: OS 40

The Parliamentary bridge was replaced in 1899 in late Georgian style, further upstream. The present Shiel Bridge was built in 1935.

10.33 Glencoe (Plate 28)   NN 252 547: OS 41

A distinctive 1930s concrete road bridge near the Kingshouse

RAILWAYS

Railways came late to Lochaber, and the most impressive features are the viaducts, the largest being built of concrete rather than stone, and at the time in the forefront of technology.

10.34 Borrodale Burn railway viaduct, Arisaig
NM 698 855: OS 40

Its central concrete arch was when it was built in 1897–1901 the largest span in the world at 127 ft 6 in (38.9 m) and 86 ft (26 m) high

10.35 Glenfinnan viaduct (Plate 27)   NM 906 808: OS 40

Built between 1897 and 1901, is the longest concrete railway bridge in Scotland, being 1,248 ft (380 m) long, and over 100 ft (30 m) high. It can be glimpsed from the main road, and the car park of the National Trust for Scotland Visitor Centre. Behind the Visitor Centre is a path up to a viewpoint. For those wishing a closer look, use the car park the other side of the river, and take a short walk up the private road which passes under the viaduct. There is also a railway museum at Glenfinnan.

10.36 Loch nam Uamh viaduct, Loch Ailort
NM 83/84 72: OS 40

Built 1897–1901 of concrete, with eight arches each with a fifty-foot (15 m) span. Both this and Glenfinnan were built by Robert MacAlpine.

10.37 The Spean Bridge–Invergarry–Fort Augustus Railway

Opened in 1903, and closed in 1946. It ran along the east side of Loch Oich, partly on the line of the old Wade Road, joining the Glasgow to Fort William line at NN 214 813: OS 41.

INNS AND HOTELS

These can be divided into traditional sites, with buildings originating in the eighteenth or early nineteenth century, though often added to later, and those which were newly built in the later nineteenth century, reflecting new routes (including railways) or new types of customer, such as sportsmen. This list contains a few examples of both types, but there are many more, though a surprisingly large number, particularly of the later ones, have been destroyed by fire.

10.38 Ardgour Inn   NN 015 637: OS 41

A classic agglomeration of buildings at a ferry point

10.39 Former inn and post office, Arisaig (Fig. 20)

NM 658 864: OS 40

Built at the same time as the Parliamentary road, finished 1812

10.40 Ballachulish Hotel   NN 050 596: OS 41

By the old ferry slip, a Gothic design by J. Honeyman, and built in 1877. Across the narrows by the other ferry slip stands the Loch Leven Hotel.

10.41 Banavie   NN 113 770: OS 41

The former Locheil Arms Hotel, built in the 1830s beside the Caledonian Canal

10.42 Clachaig Inn   NN 127 567: OS 41

Outside Glencoe village, was built in 1839. From 1843 it was a stage for coaches from Fort William through Glencoe to Central Scotland.

10.43 Glenuig Inn   NM 670 772: OS 40

Parts of which may date back to the eigtheenth century

10.44 Invergarry Hotel   NH 306 012: OS 34

Built in 1885, picturesque

10.45 Kingshouse, Glencoe (Plate 15)   NN 259 546: OS 41

Built by Caulfield in 1751, though possibly on the site of an earlier inn. Remote inns such as this might be overcrowded, or short of food. It was luck how much hospitality and comfort was available. Dorothy and William Wordsworth stayed here in 1803, when it had 'long rooms, with ranges of beds, no other furniture', and the landlady had 'no eggs, no milk, no potatoes, no loaf-bread', the peat was too damp to make a good fire, and the sheets were so damp they took ages to

Fig. 53. The Strontian Hotel (10.46)

dry by such a poor fire. Lord Teignmouth in 1836 described it as 'a solitary inn, appearing like a caravanserai in the desert'.

10.46 Strontian Hotel (Fig. 53) NM 815 614: OS 40

The centre dates from 1808, with the remains of its stables and coach-house behind

11. BATTLE SITES
(IN CHRONOLOGICAL ORDER)

11.1 The battle of Torquil's Ford, Acharacle NM 67 68: OS 40

In the twelfth century, between Somerled and the Viking Torquil

11.2 The First Battle of Inverlochy NN 118 753: OS 41

Fought close to the castle in January 1431, was one of several battles fought by James I against the supporters of Alexander, Lord of the Isles, whose power he was trying to break. But James was defeated.

11.3 The Battle of the Shirts NN 28 96: OS 34

Fought at the head of Loch Lochy in 1544, with MacDonalds and Camerons on one side against the Frasers. The day was so hot they took off their plaids and fought only wearing their shirts. Very few men survived the battle.

11.4 The Second Battle of Inverlochy NN 12 74: OS 41

Fought in February 1645, to the south-east of the castle, towards Glen Nevis. The royalist army, led by the Marquis of Montrose, had been camped south of Fort Augustus, on their way to Inverness, when they were informed by Iain Lom, the Keppoch bard, that the Covenanters, under the Marquis of Argyll, were at Inverlochy. Montrose therefore turned back and marched by hill tracks to surprise the Covenanters, and defeated them. Argyll himself watched from his galley across the Loch, and escaped.

11.5   Mulroy, near Roybridge   NN 272 827: OS 34

Was the scene of the last clan battle in Scotland, fought on 4 August 1688, and also the last recorded use of bows and arrows in battle, when the Mackintoshes, with the aid of government troops, tried unsuccessfully to seize some MacDonald land.

> Col. MacDonald, the head of a small clan, refused to pay the dues demanded from him by Mackintosh, as his superior lord. They disdained the interposition of judges and laws, and calling each his followers to maintain the dignity of the clan, fought a formal battle, in which several considerable men fell on the side of Mackintosh, without a complete victory to either. This is said to have been the last open war made between the clans by their own authority. (Samuel Johnson)

11.6   High Bridge, near Spean Bridge (Plate 13)
NN 199 819: OS 41

The site of first incident of the 1745 rising, commemorated by a cairn beside the road. On 16 August 1745 two companies of government troops on their way to Fort William were ambushed near the northern end of the bridge by 12 Keppoch MacDonalds. With a piper, and by moving around in the undergrowth, yelling and shooting, they gave the impression of being a far larger force, and the government troops retreated.

12. MONUMENTS
(IN CHRONOLOGICAL ORDER OF THE
EVENTS THEY COMMEMORATE)

12.1 Well of the Seven Heads, Invergarry (Fig. 54)
NN 304 991: OS 34

A memorial to the 'Keppoch Murders', erected in 1812 by Alasdair MacDonald of Glengarry. An unpopular MacDonald laird of Keppoch had been killed in 1663 by the neighbouring laird of Inverlair, whom he had persecuted. Iain Lom sought revenge, and eventually, two years later, persuaded another MacDonald laird to attack Inverlair. Seven men were killed in the raid. Iain Lom had their heads cut off to present to Glengarry, who had refused to help avenge the first murder. The site marks the place where the heads were washed. By the loch shore is the well. Above it stands an obelisk, topped by seven carved heads. On the base, a long inscription which starts AS A *MEMORIAL* OF THE AMPLE AND SUMMARY *VENGEANCE*, WHICH IN THE SWIFT COURSE OF *FEUDAL* JUSTICE ... OVERTOOK THE PERPETRATORS OF THE FOUL MURDER OF A MEMBER OF THE *KEPPOCH FAMILY* ...

12.2 Glencoe   NN 104 588: OS 41

'In 1884 Mrs Archibald Burns-MacDonald of Glencoe, a direct descendant of Mac Ian, erected on a picturesque knoll at Bridge of Coe, close by the ancient village of the glen, a Celtic cross to the memory of the slain. It is 18 feet in height, stands on a cairn 7 feet high, and is of dark red granite, richly carved with Runic scrolls'

Fig. 54. The top of the monument at the Well of the Seven Heads (12.1)

(*Ordnance Gazetteer*, 1894). The inscription reads: 'This cross is reverently erected in memory of MacIain, Chief of the MacDonalds of Glencoe, who fell with his people in the massacre of Glen Coe of February 1692, by his direct descendant, Ellen Burns MacDonald of Glen Coe, August 1883. Their memory liveth evermore.'

12.3 Prince's Cairn, Loch nan Uahm   NM 720 844: OS 40

Erected in 1956 to mark the spot from which the Prince embarked for France on 20 September 1746

12.4   Seven Men of Moidart   NM 703 726: OS 40

A row of beech trees on the shores of Loch Moidart, said to have been
planted soon after the failed rising of 1745–6 to commemorate the
loyal followers who came across from France with the Prince. The
trees can be viewed from a lay-by which has a cairn and information
boards.

12.5   Glenfinnan Monument (Plate 14)   NM 906 805: OS 40

Possibly designed by James Gillespie Graham, built in 1815 by
Alexander MacDonald of Glenaladale to commemorate the raising
of the standard at the start of the 1745 Jacobite rising, though it is
probably not sited on the exact spot. It does, however, command the
landscape. MacDonald died the year it was built, so it serves as a
monument to him as well. The structure was originally surrounded
by a larger circular wall. Attached to the tower was a small building,
known as the 'shooting box'. By 1824 this was in disrepair, and in the
early 1830s it was demolished and the present octagonal perimeter
wall built, and the cast-iron plaques added. In addition, the statue
of a Highlander, often misinterpreted as representing the Young
Pretender, was added on top of the tower.

According to Queen Victoria: 'At the head of the loch stands a
very ugly monument to Prince Charles Edward, looking like a sort
of lighthouse surmounted by his statue, and surrounded by a wall'.
M.E.M. Donaldson in 1920 described it as 'a fifth-rate lighthouse
surmounted by an insignificant figure of the Prince and surrounded
by a wall whose ugliness is in no way inferior to that of the column
itself'. Since 1938 the monument has been in the care of the National
Trust for Scotland. The three cast-iron plaques on the outside of the
perimeter wall bear the same words in Gaelic, Latin and English:

> On this spot, where Prince Charles Edward first raised his standard,
> on the 19th day of August 1745, when he made the daring and
> romantic attempt to recover a throne lost by the imprudence of his
> ancestors, this column is erected by Alexander MacDonald, Esq.,

of Glenaladale, to commemorate the generous zeal, the undaunted bravery, and the inviolable fidelity of his forefathers and the rest of those who fought and bled in that arduous and unfortunate enterprise. This pillar is now, alas, also become the monument of its amiable and accomplished founder, who, before it was finished. died in Edinburgh, on the sixth day of January 1815, at the early age of 28 years.

12.6 James of the Glen, Ballachulish   NN 051 595: OS 41

An old cairn (dating from 1770 or earlier), standing among forestry, marks the spot where the Appin Murder was committed (NN 031 594: OS 41), and a more modern memorial, erected in 1911, stands at the spot where James of the Glen was hanged for the crime he almost certainly did not commit. Described by M. E. M. Donaldson as 'a peculiarly hideous monument', it overlooks the south end of the Ballachulish Bridge, and can be reached by steps from the east side of the Ballachulish Hotel. One of the four guns said to have been used in the murder can be seen in the West Highland Museum, Fort William.

12.7 Cameron Obelisk, Kilmallie   NN 090 768: OS 41

In front of the church stands an enormous obelisk erected by the officers of the Gordon Highlanders, at a cost of £1,400, to commemorate Colonel John Cameron of Fassifern (1771–1815), who fell leading his regiment at the battle of Quatre Bras, just before Waterloo. The inscription is said to have been written by Sir Walter Scott. It ends with the words: 'Reader, call not his fate untimely, who, thus honoured and lamented, closed a life of fame by a death of glory'.

12.8 Commando Monument, Spean Bridge (Plate 29)
NN 207 824: OS 41

A fine bronze group of three soldiers by Scott Sutherland, commemorating the Commandos killed during the Second World

War, and overlooking the area in which many of them received their training. This impressive monument was unveiled by the Queen Mother in 1952.

FURTHER READING, AND
BOOKS QUOTED IN THE TEXT

Anon., *'Mountain Moor and Loch' illustrated by Pen and Pencil on the routs of the West Highland Railway*, London, 1894.

Anon., *The Steam Boat Companion and Stranger's Guide to the Western Islands and Highlands of Scotland*, Glasgow, 1820.

Armit, Ian, *Celtic Scotland*, Historic Scotland, London, 1997.

Barnett, T. Ratcliffe, *The Land of Locheil and the Magic West*, Edinburgh, 1927.

Boswell, James, *Journey of a Tour to the Hebrides with Samuel Johnson* (R.W. Chapman, ed.), Oxford, 1970.

Bowman, J.E., *The Highlands and Islands: A Nineteenth-Century Tour*, Gloucester, 1826.

Brown, Rev. Thomas, *Annals of the Disruption*, Edinburgh, 1884.

Burt, S., *Letters from a Gentleman in the North of Scotland . . .*, London, 1754.

Cameron, A.D., *The Caledonian Canal*, Edinburgh, 1994.

Campbell, Marion, *Argyll, The Enduring Heartland*, London, 1977.

Crawford, Barbara, *Scandinavian Scotland*, Leicester, 1987.

Defoe, D., *A Tour through the whole island of Great Britain*, G.D.H. Cole and D.C. Browning (eds), 2 vols, London, 1962.

Defoe, D., *A Tour through the whole island of Great Britain*, 8th edn, with additions by various authors, 4 vols, London, 1778.

Donaldson, M.E.M., *Wanderings in the Western Highlands and Islands . . .*, Paisley, 1920.

Donaldson, M.E.M., *Further Wanderings – mainly in Argyll*, Paisley, 1926.

Duff, David (ed.), *Queen Victoria's Highland Journals*, Exeter, 1983.

Fairley, R. (ed.), *Jemima: the paintings and memoirs of a Victorian lady*, Edinburgh, 1988.

Gaskell, Philip, *Morvern Transformed: A Highland Parish in the Nineteenth Century*, Cambridge, 1968.

Gifford, John, *The Buildings of Scotland: Highlands and Islands*, London, 1992.

Groome, F.H., *Ordnance Gazetteer of Scotland*, 6 vols, London, 1894.

Haldane, A.R.B., *New Ways through the Glens, Highland Road, Bridge and Canal Makers of the early Nineteenth Century*, Colonsay, 1962.

Haldane, A.R.B., *The Drove Roads of Scotland*, Edinburgh, 1997.

Hogg, James, *Highland Tours*, reprinted Hawick, 1981.

Johnson, Samuel, *Journey to the Western Islands of Scotland* (R.W. Chapman, ed.), Oxford, 1970.

Kilgour, William T., *Lochaber in War and Peace*, Paisley, 1908.

Knox, John, *A Tour through the Highlands of Scotland and the Hebride Isles, in 1786*, London, 1787.

Leyden, John, *Journal of a Tour in the Highlands and Western Islands of Scotland in 1800*, Edinburgh, 1903.

London & North Eastern Railway, *The Story of the West Highland*, 1944, reprinted 2001.

MacCulloch, Donald, *Romantic Lochaber*, 2nd edn, Edinburgh, 1948.

Macculloch, John, *The Highlands and Western Isles of Scotland*, 4 vols, London, 1824.

MacDonald, Rev. Charles, *Moidart: or, among the Clanranalds*, Oban, 1889.

MacGibbon, D. and Ross, T., *The Castellated and Domestic Architecture of Scotland*, 5 vols, Edinburgh, 1887-92.

Maclean, Fiona, *Around Lochaber*, Stroud, 1996.

Maclean, Lorraine, *Discovering Inverness-shire*, Edinburgh, 1988.

Macleod, Norman, *Reminiscences of a Highland Parish*, reprinted as *Morvern, A Highland Parish* (I. Thornber, ed.), Edinburgh, 2002.

Mitchell, Joseph, *Reminiscences of my Life in the Highlands* (1883), I. Robertson (ed), 2 vols, Newton Abbot, 1971.

Morvern Heritage Society, *Exploring Morvern*, privately published, 2004.

Murray, D., *The York Buildings Company: a chapter in Scotch history*, Glasgow, 1883.

[New] Statistical Account of Scotland, VII, Renfrew – Argyle, Edinburgh, 1845.

[New] Statistical Account of Scotland, XIV, Inverness – Ross & Cromarty, Edinburgh, 1845.

[Old] Statistical Account of Scotland 1791–1799, vol. VIII, Argyll (mainland), Sir J. Sinclair (ed.), facsimile edn, D.J. Withrington and I.R. Grant (eds), Wakefield, 1983.

[Old] Statistical Account of Scotland 1791–1799, vol. XVII, Inverness-shire, Ross and Cromarty, Sir J. Sinclair (ed.), facsimile edn, D.J. Withrington and I.R. Grant (eds), Wakefield, 1981.

Pennant, Thomas, *A Tour in Scotland 1769*, Warrington, 1774.

Pennant, Thomas, *A Tour in Scotland and Voyage to the Hebrides 1772*, reprinted Edinburgh, 1998.

Pigot and Co's New Commercial Directory of Scotland for 1825–6, London and Manchester.

Richards, Eric, *The Highland Clearances: People, Landlords and Rural Turmoil*, Edinburgh, 2000.

Ritchie, Graham & Harman, Mary, *Exploring Scotland's Heritage: Argyll and the Western Isles*, RCAHMS, Edinburgh, 1985.

Rixson, Denis, *Arisaig and Morar: A History*, East Linton, 2002.

Robson, James, *General View of the Agriculture in the County of Argyll, and the Western Part of Inverness-shire*, London, 1794.

Royal Commission on the Ancient and Historical Monuments of Scotland, *Argyll: an inventory of the monuments, vol 3, Mull, Tiree, Coll and Northern Argyll*, Edinburgh, 1980.

Salmond, J.B., *Wade in Scotland*, Edinburgh and London, 2nd edn, 1938.

Stewart, Alexander, *Nether Lochaber: the natural history, legends, and fold-lore of the West Highlands*, Edinburgh, 1883.

Stewart, Alexander, *Twixt Ben Nevis and Glencoe: the natural history, legends, and folk-lore of the West Highlands*, Edinburgh, 1885.

Sunart Oakwoods Research Group, *The Sunart Oakwoods: A Report on their History and Archaeology*, privately published, 2001.

Tabraham, Chris and Grove, Doreen, *Fortress Scotland and the Jacobites*, Historic Scotland, London, 1995.

Third Statistical Account, County of Argyll, C.M. MacDonald (ed.), Glasgow, 1961 (Kilchoan, Rev. N.G. MacDonald; Acharacle, Rev. D. MacPhail; Strontian, A. Cameron; Ardgour, Rev. A.D. MacLean; Morvern, Rev. H. MacSween).

Third Statistical Account, County of Inverness, H. Barron (ed.), Edinburgh, 1985 (Arisaig and Moidart, Rev. D. Macintosh Logan; Glenelg, Rev. N. MacDonald; Kilmallie, Rev. A. Robertson *et al.*; Kilmonivaig, Rev. A. Mackinnon).

Weir, Marie, *Ferries in Scotland*, Edinburgh, 1988.

Weyndling, Walter, *Ferry Tales of Argyll and the Isles*, Stroud, 1996.

Wickham-Jones, Caroline, *Scotland's First Settlers*, London, 1994.